TERROR

IN OUR

MIDST

ABOUT THE POET

Suprio Ghosh is a poet, a songwriter, a cartoonist and a short story writer.

He identifies himself as a common man and a realist who is a citizen of the 'global village', which has been divided by negative thinking, motives, selfishness and more. His goal is to help comprehend these lethal and horrible realities. He believes that a cure is possible through a unity of purpose and honest cooperation among all nations.

Ghosh has also authored How To Stop Wars??? which is available on the Amazon Kindle store.

TERROR IN OUR MIDST

Suprio Ghosh

ZORBA BOOKS

Published in India by Zorba Books, 2018

Website: www.zorbabooks.com
Email: info@zorbabooks.com

ISBN 978-93-87456-43-3

Zorba Books Pvt. Ltd.(opc)
Gurgaon, INDIA

Printed at Repro Knowledgecast Limited, Thane

DEDICATION

This book is dedicated to Mona Lisa,
my pet and my best friend
who was always with me
when I wrote this book
and has sadly passed away.

A NOTE FROM THE POET

The poems in this little book may be read individually or in the sequence the poet has arranged them.

The poems in this little book are to enlighten us about barbarism, terrorism, militancy and communal violence which are different faces of the same evil.

This evil has to be totally eradicated. The saying, 'United we stand, divided we fall' is very true in this case also. All nations of our world must unite with all their might, to be able to eradicate this evil which spreads at a lightning pace, and is trying to conquer the civilized world.

The reality of terrorism is a horrendous one, truly horrific in nature. Methods used by terrorists while interacting with the concept of a civilized society possessing democratic and human values are monstrously beastly, barbaric, brutal and gruesome.

Acts of terror take place so that the perpetrators are able to create panic among the population and eventually dominate.

The horror created by acts of terror like beheading, pillage, hangings in public squares, mass executions, ethnic cleansing of minorities, rape and destruction of other cultures are barbaric in nature and terrify the sane, the normal, the peace loving and the civilized.

Something must be done to stop and eradicate this evil. To be able to do something to eradicate this evil unity among all nations is a must.

A terrorist has no religion. They only misuse religion by insisting that a distorted version, what they promote, is the correct one and use terror tactics to force the population to follow it or else. Neither do they understand nor do they respect international boundaries. All nations should shred their old notions and beliefs of who is friend and who is foe and realize that the only foe is the one that is barbaric and wants to take over the world through their terror tactics.

It's a new world order now and evil barbaric concepts are becoming monstrous, spreading their tentacles to take over anything civilized or cultured.

We must wake up and accept this reality we live in now. Earlier it was a different world order, nations had friends and foes and each trying to dominate the other with power of any kind, military, economic, flashy goods, sex, color of skin or goods of material value.

A new world order has and is being created, transformation is taking place at a very fast pace. A new school of thought has been created. We helped in its creation when we were doing it to each other.

The new world order says or rather dictates a new school of thought that demands obedience and strict acceptance and adherence to its norms and beliefs and lifestyle.

A new class of slaves is taking birth through efficient and effective brain washing techniques. They are cruel, brutal, barbaric, beastly and insane in nature and impose their master's belief.

Many nations are turning a blind eye to this reality, as

though it doesn't exist.

Words, actions, cooperation levels or non- cooperation as such clearly show that they are blind to this reality or turn a blind eye to this reality, simply because they live in the old world order of friends and foes and insist that they have to look first into national interest, security and strategic depth. This is insane, primitive and self centric in a lunatic way and a folly.

There is no place for traditional external affairs policies in the new world order which is insane, barbaric and knows no national boundaries.

They want to take over the world and impose their beliefs. The obvious fact is that they will spare no one.

Do we want to be slaves of the new world order that is emerging at a lightning pace? Or, do we want to stop it and eradicate it?

The answer is obvious. No one wants to be a slave so we have to stop the terror machine and eradicate it.

If this is true all nations must unite with all their intelligence and might to be able to do the obvious and to further utilize the cooperation level to cure many Global woes.

The poet uses the Oxford English dictionary.

POET: -SUPRIO GHOSH

A NOTE FROM THE POET

1. THE GAME OF DEATH

2. TERROR IN OUR MIDST 1.

3. THE MADNESS OF MAN

4. THE MUMBAI CARNAGE

5. TAME THE EVIL

6. SENSELESS ACTS

7. STATE SPONSERED HORROR

8. UNPREDICTBALE SUICIDE BOMBERS

9. INSANE ACTS

10. UNASWERED QUESTIONS

11. NEW NAMES FOR THE OLD

12. COMMUNAL VOILENCE & BYPRODUCTS

13. COMMUNAL HORROR

14. ERADICATING COMMUNAL VOILENCE

15. IT HAPPENS TOO OFTEN

16. CRUSH MINDSETS LIKE THE TALIBAN

17. INFANTILE OR IMBECILE

18. THE MUDDLED EAST 1.

19. TERROR IN OUR MIDST 2.

20. THE TERRORISTS

21. TERRORISM TODAY

22. WHO WILL BELL THE CAT???

23. AWAKEN OH! MEDIA

24. I HOPE WE LEARN FROM THE PAST

25. GROW UP

26. THINK ABOUT IT

27. WHY???

28. IS THE MEDIA, HELPING THE TERRORISTS???

29. TERRORISTS EXPOLT COMMUNAL DISCORD, DISHARMONY & TENSIONS

30. WHO ARE THEY? WHO MAKE THE MOB???

31. THE MAD MOTHER MIND

32. MEANINGLESS TREATIES

33. WAKE UP ALL NATIONS

34. PLEASE LISTEN ALL NATIONS

35. IT'S TIME TO PONDER

36. ERADICATING EVIL 'IS'

37. TWO POWERFUL TENTACLES OF TERROR

38. THEY HURT THEIR OWN

39. THE MUDDLED EAST 2.

40. HAVE THE 'IS' LOST THE WAR?

41. ANOTHER INVISIBLE ENEMY

42. TOUGH ON TERRORISM

43. STILL THERE IS TIME

44. BETTER POLICIES PLEASE

45. UNITE AND COOPERATE HONESTLY

46. WE HAVE TO

47. TERROR IN OUR MIDST 3.

48. WHO IS RESPONSIBLE?

49. DEMOLISH THE TERROR MACHINE

50. PLEASE REALIZE AND COOPERATE

51. UPROOTING TERRORISM

52. ALL NATIONS UNITE

53. WHAT A WASTE OF BRAINWASHING
    TECHNIQUES

54. BETTER STRATAGIES PLEASE

55. LET'S TRY COOPRATION

56. HOW???

57. DEAR GOD

1. THE GAME OF DEATH

The train was blasted
Off the track
By professionals
Who, knew the knack

Most coaches lay topsy-turvy
Five coaches were mangled
Evil vibrations filled the air
As though someone was being strangled

Shrieks and fits of weeping
Filled the air
Painful cries
Could be heard everywhere

Like the agony of the animal
Caught in a rabbits snare
It was chaos everywhere
Confusion, reigned the air

This game of death
Why did they play?
Who planned this horror?
Who financed this day?

Who benefits from such barbarism?
Who gains from its execution?
Who sets such evil?
Into, such deadly motion
We must get rid of
This horrible evil mind

Suprio Ghosh

Corner them with tact
And eventually, them grind

We must nab those who plan
And participate in such acts of terror
We must nab those who destroy peace & harmony
And indulge in such acts of horror

It's a Global Village now
All nations ought to cooperate in this fight
We need unity among all nations to build an invincible shield
By utilizing all their intelligence and might

Suprio Ghosh

2. TERROR IN OUR MIDST 1.

The terrorists struck once again
Did they gain?
Cashing in
On, someone else's pain
This madness is
The work of the insane

Endless strikes by terrorists
Seems to rule the day
Endless strikes by terrorists
It seems as though they're here to stay
Unpredictable strikes by terrorists
The present and the future look grey

How do we?
Rid ourselves of this ill
Do we need unity, conviction?
And an iron will
Cooperation among all nations
We have to instil

Let's do it quickly
Before it gets out of hand
We need unity and cooperation
And not a magic wand
All nations must unite
We have a tough fight at hand.

Suprio Ghosh

3. THE MADNESS OF MAN

Evening came bringing with her
A barbaric turbulent storm
A crystal clear display
Of mans most hideous form

One community tried to annihilate another
At least hurt them as much as one can
Wicked, barbaric was the display
Madness of a beast called man

A minority community
Was attacked the other day
Most died, some seriously injured
Though some did get away

Insanity ruled the day
It was mayhem all the way
Wild beasts from the jungles seemed tame
Humanity lost the day

D-2

Suprio Ghosh

4. THE MUMBAI CARNAGE

The Mumbai carnage ought to be
An eye opener for one & all
The policy of 'Bleed India with a thousand cuts'
Ought to be squashed, once & for all

Citizens of many nations
This carnage consumed
Many died & many more were wounded
The terrorists were well groomed

They knew when and where to strike
And who all would be there
They wanted to paralyze India's financial nerve centre
So that to do biz with India none would dare

They thought no trace of the perpetuators would be left
No information about who planned it all
They didn't expect one of theirs to be caught alive
And spill the beans, about it all

The international community knows about all this
And try to impose their dictates
But the state that sponsors such horrors
Tries to distort and hide the facts

State sponsored terrorism
Can't be concealed for a long time
State sponsored terrorism
Is an abhorrable crime

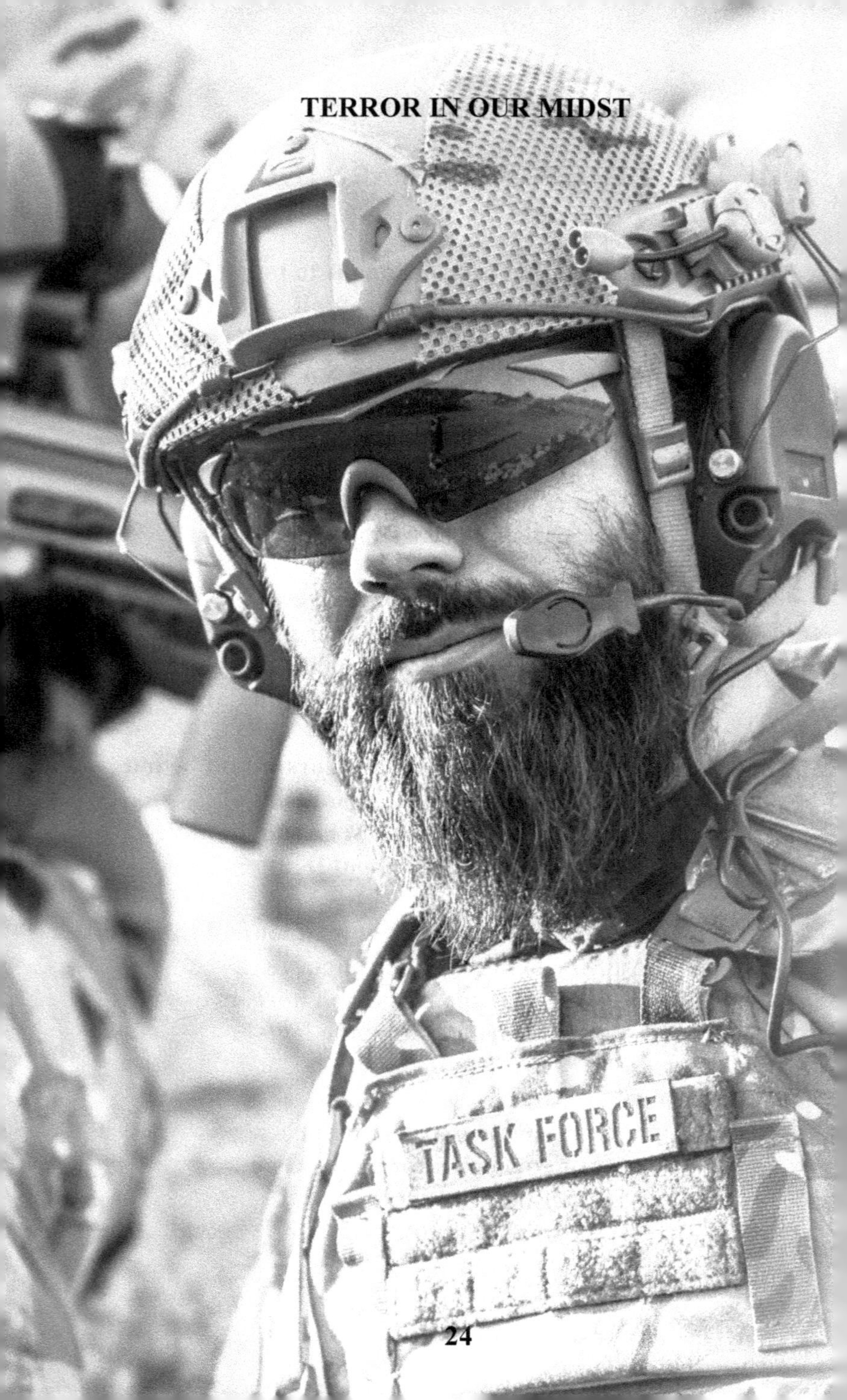
TASK FORCE

Suprio Ghosh

Strict sanctions ought to be imposed
On nations committing such deed
They ought to be ostracised
There is a need

They ought to be compelled to realize
That peace & harmony is our Global Village's need
That our Global Village doesn't need
Proxy wars, terrorism, barbarism, deceit & greed

Suprio Ghosh

5. TAME THE EVIL

Communal violence, militancy, terrorism
Are different faces
Of the same
Brand of evil
That destroys
Lives
Lifestyles
Infrastructure
Economy
Tolerance
Peace and harmony
Whipping
Happiness
Progress & prosperity
To their knees
This evil
We must tame

TERROR IN OUR MIDST

Suprio Ghosh

6. SENSELESS ACTS

It was a day
Of festive delight
Everything seemed
So gay and bright
Frolic and colours
Engrossed the sight
None knew
Of the coming plight

People were there
By the score
The market was crowded
Couldn't ask for more
A mad rush was on
To empty every store
They shoved & pushed each other
To be at the fore

There was a loud bang
Deafened every ear
Everything became silent
Engulfed by a sense of fear
Slowly, the wails started
From not far and very near
Wails, sobs and shrieks
Was all that one could hear

Then utter chaos
Reigned the day
A mad rush was on
To get away

Suprio Ghosh

Stumbling over the bloodied corpses
On the way
Paranoia reigned
They did not want to stay

Mutilated body parts
Lay here and there
The blood splattered injured
Were wailing for care
Some were shocked
With an empty stare
Blooded corpses
Lay everywhere

The market was partially flattened
Some shop were ablaze
Peace and tranquillity shattered
Everyone was in a daze
The frolic and gaiety
Was just a phase
Everything seemed to be
In a chaotic maze

Goods, infrastructure and resources
Were gutted & down the drain
Making small traders bankrupt
Never reaped an ideological gain
Destroying many harmonious lives
By spreading terror and pain
Depriving families of breadwinners
Are policies, of the insane

Suprio Ghosh

Why did the terrorists?
Commit this insane deed
What did they achieve?
What was the need?
Among common citizen
They sowed the seed
Doubts, suspicion and paranoia
They managed to breed

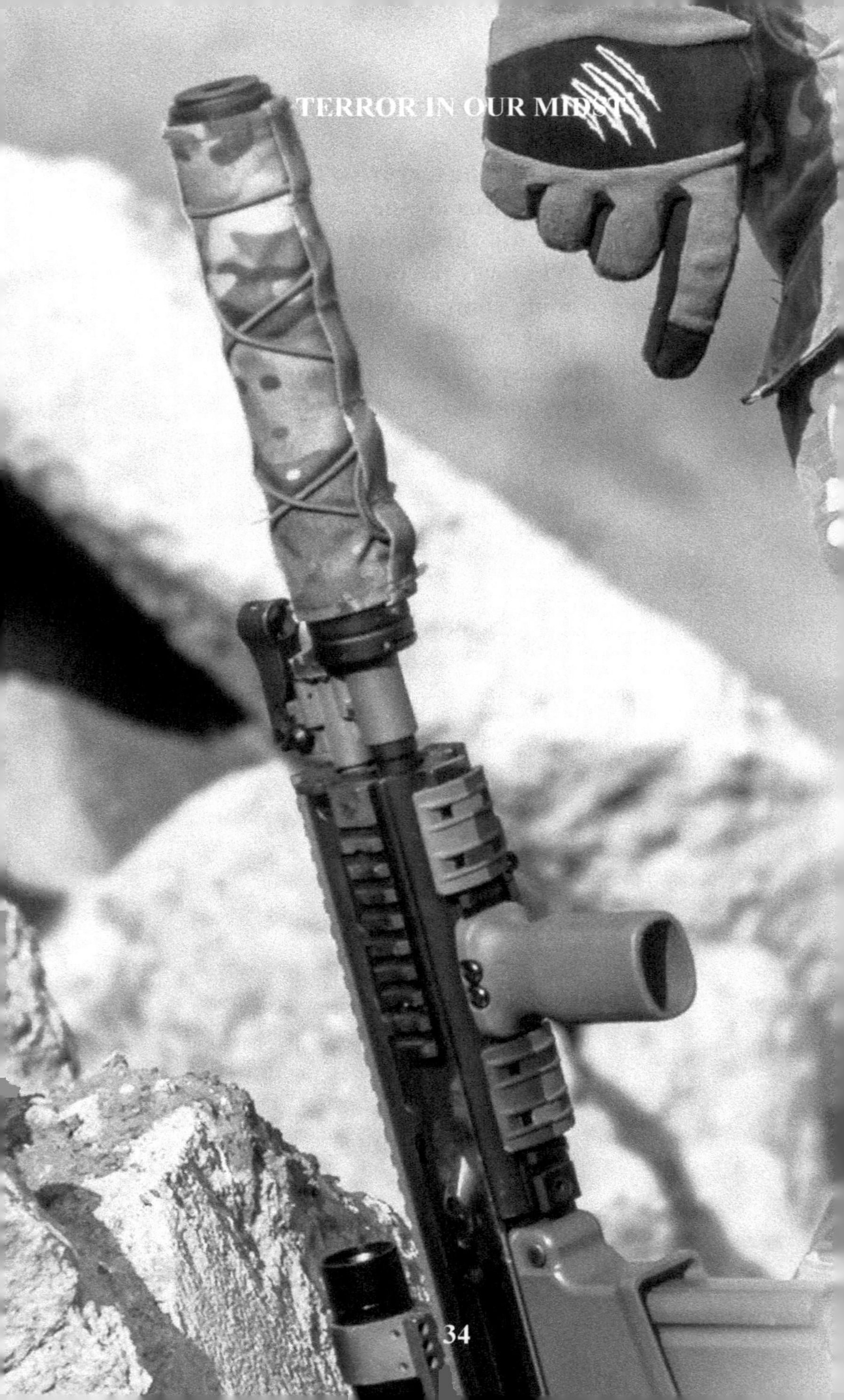

Suprio Ghosh

7. STATE-SPONSERED HORROR

Terrorism is a diabolic reality
The newspapers scream everyday
Even war and its irrational ways
Is, the cause of the chaos of today

How do we cure this turmoil?
Who are the ones to blame?
Is it the developed nations?
Who, indulge in hypocrisy, sans shame

Power they seek
At any cost
Progress is stunted
Lives are lost

Fear, pain and chaos
Reigns lives night and day
Normal lives are shattered
Survival is a fight, each day

Nations promoting weapons industries
Are the ones, to blame
Landmine production hasn't yet been banned
It's really a crying shame

They produce lethal weapons
And export them to the insane
They justify their actions
By labelling it, an economic gain

TERROR IN OUR MIDST

If we don't sell
They will buy somewhere else
With such rationale they justify
While their 'Economic might' swells

Exporting them to prosper
To finance more production
To support future R&D
Never a chance of any reduction

They say that they are civilized
And uphold human rights & dignity
Who are they trying to fool?
While promoting such revolting insanity

The UN should intervene
Ban weapons, ban wars
A universal army
Can heal many scars

Negotiating settlements
In a sane & an amicable way
Can eradicate insecurity, revive harmony
And bring in a happy sway
We have to eradicate
From its roots today
The menace of terrorism
Come what may

Who provides the ideology!
Brainwashing, training and motivation
Finance, logistics & support
Safe shelters and direction

Suprio Ghosh

Organized terrorism
Can't survive today
Without state sponsorship
To pave the way

Terrorism knows no boundaries
They should realize
Curbing terrorism in all its forms
Is only sane and wise

Terrorism is a destabilizing factor
'It' we must eradicate
Their financiers, ideologues, guardians
And the sleeper cells who wait

To terrorize & cause mayhem
Like unleashed maniacs
Destroying harmony, peace, progress
Using propaganda to distort facts
State sponsored terrorism
Must be defeated
Such unholy patronage
Must be incapacitated

Isolate the state
That encourages such insanity
Coerce them to transform
We have to save humanity

We have to save sane beings
From the terrorists maniacal ways
If we can achieve it
We will surely see safer days

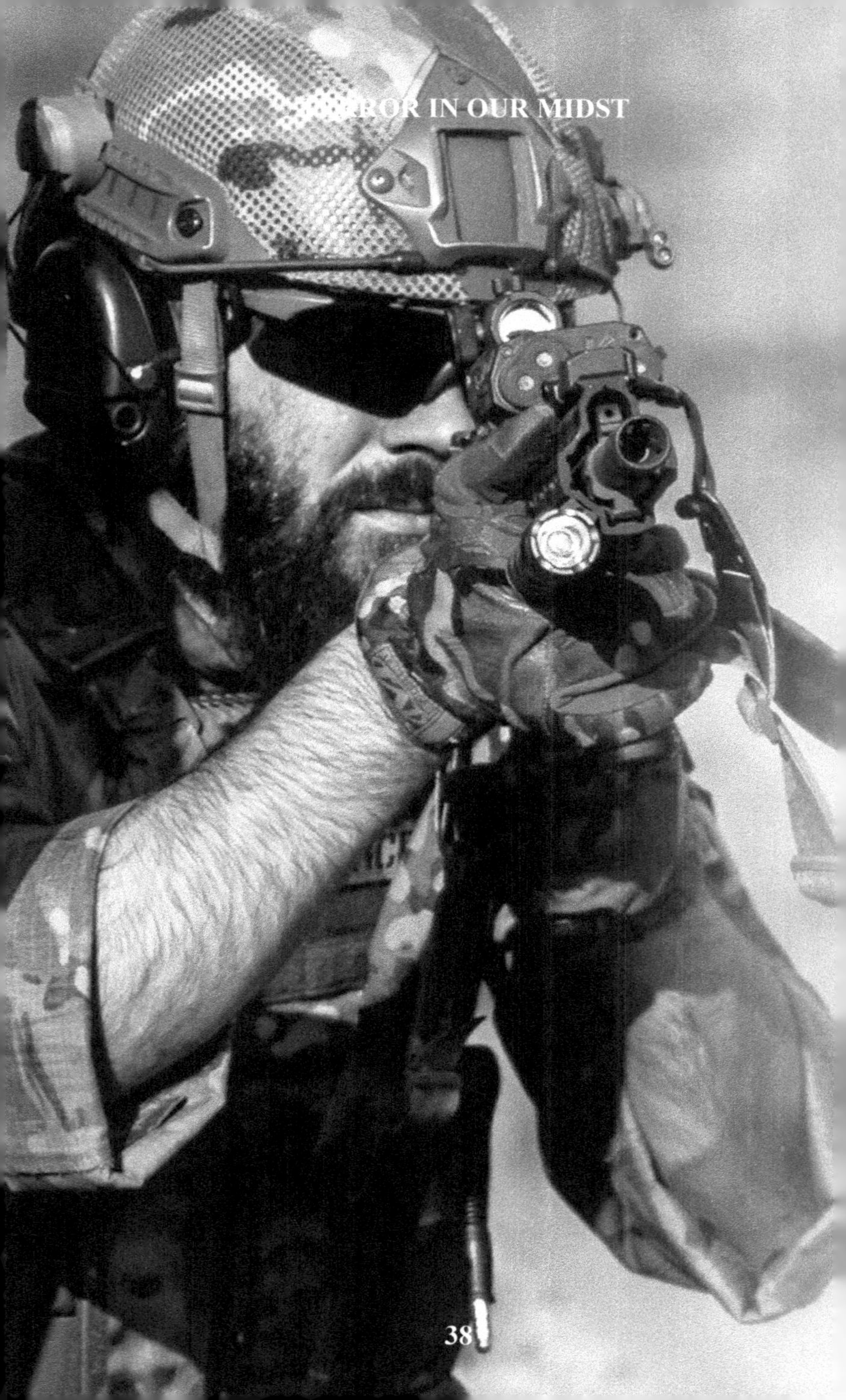

8. UNPREDICTABLE SUICIDE BOMBERS

Beware the suicide bombers
Strike yet again
Causing mutilations, destruction
Death, agony and pain
They do it willingly
Not accepting, views of the sane

Terror they spread
Ruthless, senseless horror & pain
Paranoia they cultivate
So that their 'Mad masters' gain
Turmoil they breed
An act of the insane

What makes them go?
The insane way
What makes them feel?
Their acts are OK
Is this strange & wicked creed?
Here to stay

What gives one, the courage?
To take one's own life
Have they no reason to live?
Have they no respect for life?
Don't, they believe, life's beautiful?
If it's without strain, stress or strife

Suprio Ghosh

Dangerous times
Dangerous games
Paranoia hovers
The insane reigns
Indoctrinated by mad masters
Martyrdom, he thinks he claims

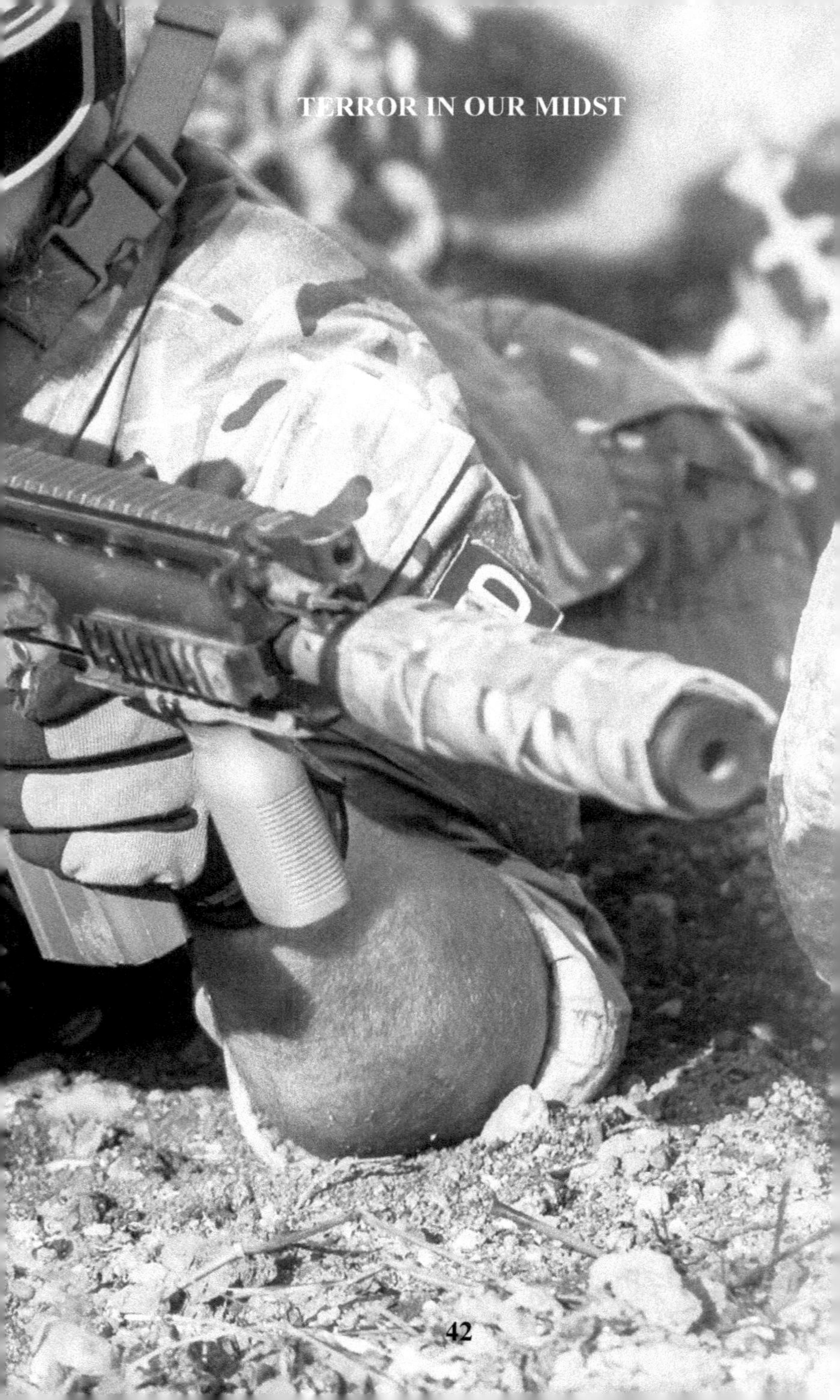

Suprio Ghosh

9. INSANEACTS

They blew up a train
The other day
When to work, ordinary people
Were on their way
With no inclination, that horror
On their path lay

The tracks were mangled
The coaches thrown wide
The train lay topsy-turvy
For the passengers, a deathly ride
Many were seriously injured
And an equal number died

It was a similar situation
In a market yesterday
They target night clubs, resorts & schools
And where people go to pray
Monsters seeking soft targets
While 'God is great', they bray

Why do the mad masters?
Commit such abhorrable deed
Is respect for life and the living?
Not a part of their creed
Their malicious propaganda causing dementia in the young
Suicide bombers, among the young they breed
Propaganda, indoctrination, training
Weapons & ammunition by the lots
How do they finance?
Such massive costs

Suprio Ghosh

With misinterpreted religion and propaganda
The fish for adults and tiny tots

All nations ought to unite & cooperate
To eradicate such abhorrable evil
They must honestly share their intelligence & might
To save the peace loving, the sane & the civil
This is the 21st century now
There ought to be no room for such evil

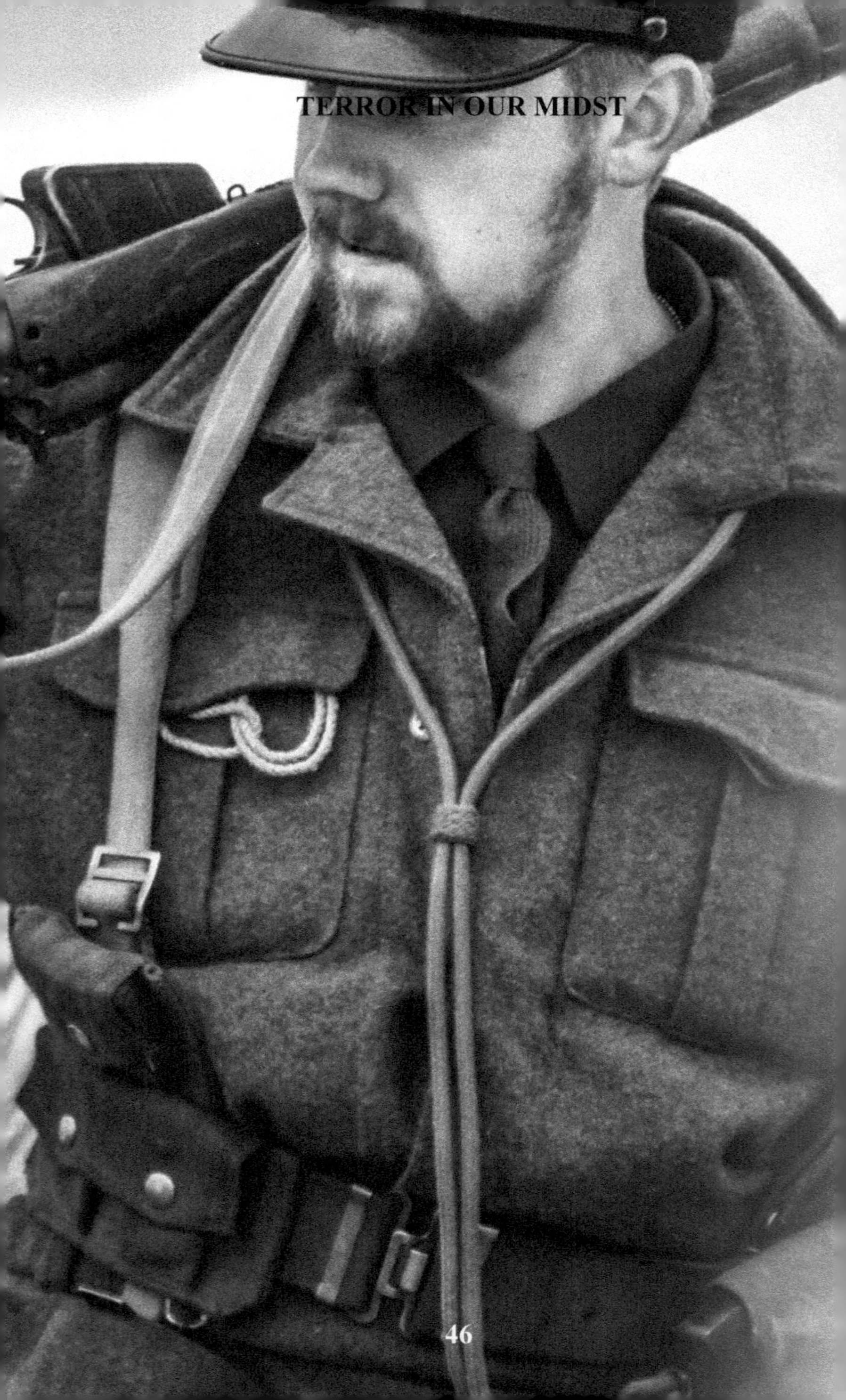

10. UNASWERED QUESTIONS

Different faiths lived in harmony
In the town not far away
One market to cater to the needs of all
Everyone went there in a happy sway

Some went to buy vegetables
Some cigarettes, some stationary and more
Some went to do window shopping
To enjoy the display at every store

The market was like any other
With many shops, some large & some small
With crowds strolling, standing or shopping
Attracted by the colourful call

A meeting place for many
Like any other market place
Everyone in their best attire
Displaying vanity or beauty and grace

It had become a daily affair
As far back as one could remember
Through all seasons and weather
Hot June, harsh rains or cold December

Till the bombs exploded
On that dreadful eve
Killing and critically wounding many
What did the militants achieve?

Suprio Ghosh

Most shops were destroyed
Some have started again
The crowds are no longer there
What did the militants gain?

Harming the common man or ruining small traders
Never helped a political cause
The militants are insane
Their path, full of flaws

Paranoia they managed to breed
Suspicion looms in the air
Chaos they managed to create
Serenity, beyond repair

TERROR IN OUR MIDST

11. NEW NAMES FOR THE OLD

Terrorism, militancy & communal violence
Are one & the same
Each one lethal & destructive
Sanity, rationality and serenity they maim
Obstructing peace, progress, growth & happiness
What a shame? What a shame?
Who is to blame?
Who is to blame?

Militancy, communal violence & terrorism
Senseless, ruthless acts
Each, the byproduct of
Belief in distorted facts
Each one brutal & barbaric
Each one motivated, senseless acts
What policy, ought one, apply
So that their cadre retracts

12. COMMUNAL VIOLENCE & BYPRODUCTS

Communal violence
Spreading pain
Destroying harmony
Negating gain

Negating progress
Wrecking a lot more
Trust, love, harmony, infrastructure & financial stability
Which reality ought to be at the fore?

Spewing venom, they create
Frenzied mob violence & hate
With propaganda they brainwash us
Trying viciously, to change our fate

Breeding hatred, instigating violence
The byproduct, instability, inability, horror & pain
Insane, ego-maniacal ideologies instigate
Policies, that annihilate & create endless pain.

Suprio Ghosh

13. COMMUNAL HORROR

Along with night came nightmare
The byproduct unimaginable pain
One community assailed another
Barbaric, terrifying, horrible & insane

Six hundred descended, upon on a sleepy village
Carrying axes, iron rods and swords
Yelling like beasts, though chanting God's name
They descended like Gingez Khan's hordes

Fearful yells
Pierced the calm night
Frightful vibrations
A hostile and deadly sight

They came like monsters
Upon the sleepy village
Their intention was quite clear
Ravage, kill, rape & pillage

They pierced, hacked and cut
Animal, man, woman & child
They unleashed barbaric fury
Like mad beasts from the wild

They broke down doors
And walls that were stout
They barged into houses
And dragged shrieking inhabitants out

TERROR IN OUR MIDST

They descended like evil
No escape for the feeble or the stout
They pillaged, ravaged and raped
They were wicked, brutal, barbaric & lout

Kill them, cut them
Some of them yelled
While insignias depicting their God
In their hands they held

The others echoed
We shall, we must
In the name of our God
In him we trust

Annihilate the nonbeliever
They aren't fit to live
Our God is true, theirs is false
They don't deserve to live

Different religions
Traditions and creed
Where harmony once prevailed
Why did this hatred breed?
Why did this hatred breed???
That turned man into a 'Mad beast'
Do we? Label him 'Wicked' or 'Terrible'
'Viscously insane' at least

Few in each community
For personal power & gain
Conceive & execute barbaric plans
Create chaos, horror & pain

Suprio Ghosh

For personal profit
To create a fearful name
To dictate as per whims & fancy
The ultimate, of this barbaric game

Doesn't man know it is evil?
To mutilate, kill or maim other beings
Don't they know what their religion teaches?
Or do they prefer, misinterpreted sayings

No religion
Teaches hatred
Each says
Life is sacred

Sane voices in a community
Teach harmony
Evil voices in a community
Teach disharmony

Why does, once a sane mind?
Become a tentacle of such barbarism
Why does, once a sane mind?
Become a slave to such maniacal egotism

Communal disharmony & violence
Destroys happy harmonious lifestyles
Creating fear, suspicion, distrust
No more happiness or smiles

No more cooperation
No harmonious interaction
No more positive growth
No sense of a healthy direction

Suprio Ghosh

Harming one and all
Harming the nation
No more cooperative ability
A catastrophic situation

Oh! Lord, help us, get rid of
Communal violence, disharmony & hate
Oh! Lord help us, change our
Bent of mind, sense of being & fate

TERROR IN OUR MIDST

Suprio Ghosh

14. ERADICATING COMMUNAL VIOLENCE

How do we stop communal violence?
How do we stop this shame?
It stunts our growth, hinders progress
And makes our exchequer lame

How do we stop this senseless destruction?
This senseless violence and hate
How do we transform the mindset?
This surely, can't be our fate

I'm sure this is a passing phase
A part of 'The learning game'
But now it's time to eradicate
This blot, this 'National shame'

It's about time we transformed the mindset
Creating a harmonious awareness level
It's about time we created sane citizen
Who are wise, progressive and civil?

Who, care for their motherland
Who are, gentle and sane
Who, mind their own affairs
And are for 'No one' a bane

Who preserve, national property
The heritage, the culture
The harmony, tolerance and brotherhood
Which tradition teaches us to nurture

Suprio Ghosh

We don't need fanatics
Who distort, thus destroy
Who, for personal satisfaction, rob?
Everyone's freedom and joy

Suprio Ghosh

15. IT HAPPENS TOO OFTEN

Though the mourning period was long over
The village was still sad
Though the wails and cries had stopped long back
The situation was just as bad

Empty stares greeted visitors
Numb beings no longer communicative
Having suffered the ultimate loss
Numb beings no longer receptive

Depression had set in on this village
That was once happy & gay
Till some militants struck not long ago
Inviting grief & despair to stay

They had lined up all the male folks
Along a barren field
Shot them all dead, ruthlessly
What did the gruesome act yield?

It was an obscure village
Their lives far away from politics
No knowledge of urban living
Or of any of the, 'Civilized dirty tricks'

No knowledge of government policies
Or matters that effect the nation
No knowledge of financial policies
Or interest in any political situation

Suprio Ghosh

Far away from civilization
They lived in peace & harmony
Worked hard to maintain their environment
The output, a visual symphony

Always kind to visitors
Never ever an evil thought
They never imagined, such horror existed
Which the militants had brought

What did the militants achieve?
What did the militants gain?
How do they justify such acts?
They are absolutely insane

Blood thirsty killers
Spreading death misery and pain
Terrorizing the local populace
Do they from such mayhem gain?

Only through the media
Cause it sensationalizes such brutal acts
Terrorizing the nation with gory details
And brutal visual facts
It's time the media became mature
And boycotted this type of news
Maybe the bare minimum coverage
And lots of critical reviews

Evolving new policies & strategies
To defeat the terrorizing insane
And not glorifying evil deeds
Is an act of the sane

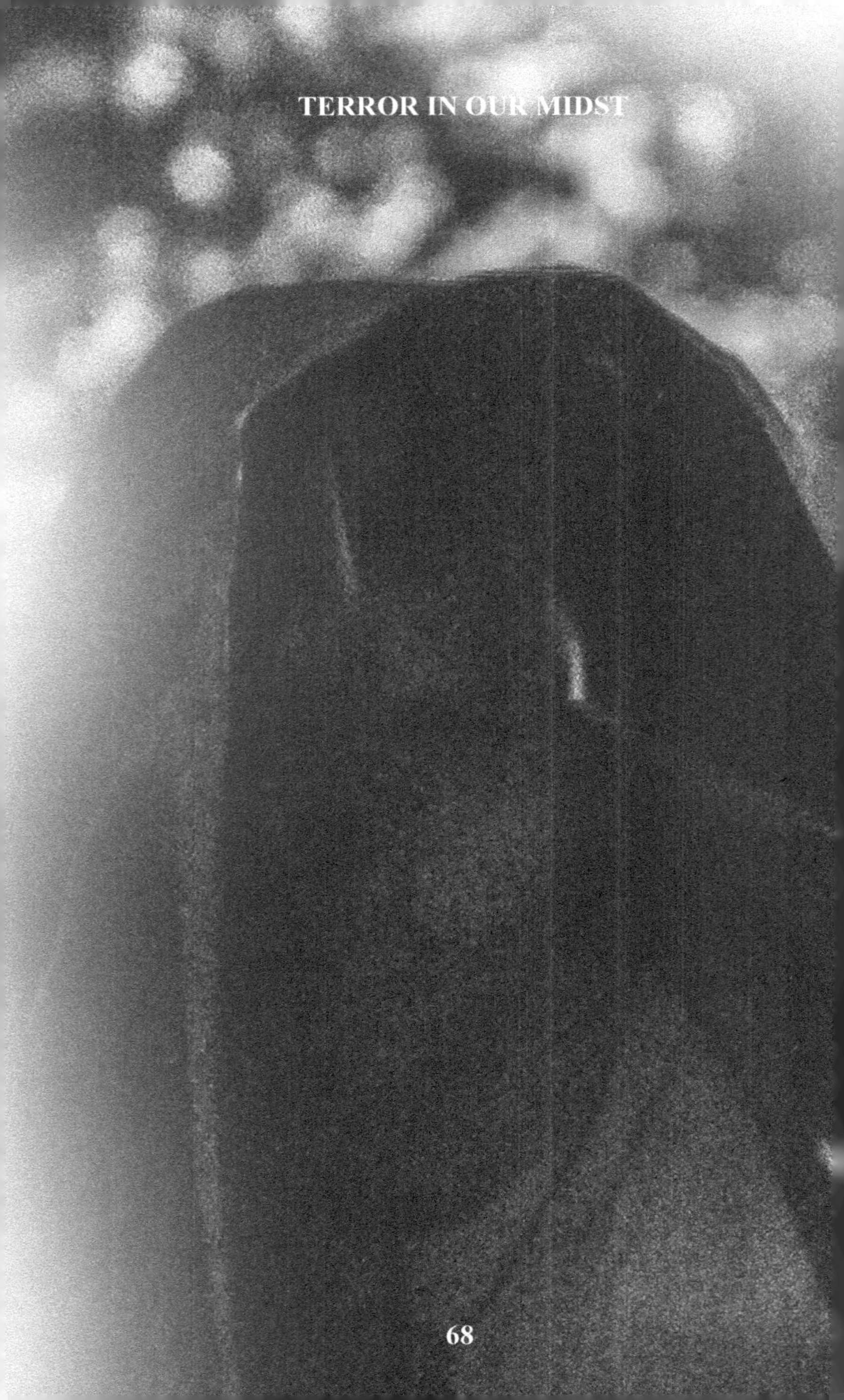

16. CRUSH MINDSETS LIKE THE TALIBAN

Massive destructive power
Lies within their reach
'Personal wealth' is created, while
One must sacrifice they teach
While promoting, death and destruction
Words of God, they preach

Misinterpreting, the sacred text
For 'Personal ambition' and gain
Misinterpreting words like sanity, love
To spread 'Death and pain'
Misusing the bondage of, a common faith
To coax and cajole, the sane

Narcotics trade, blackmail and protection money
The source of their, magical financing
Credit worthiness with 'Gun runners'
Keeps their armoury shining?
Hordes of 'Brainwashed cadre'
To commit evil deeds, at their bidding

Their networksare well entrenched
All over the globe
'Brainwashed cadre', protecting them
The game of the 'Deceptive robe'
Among the thousands a rare one is caught
Even though the agencies probe

17. INFANTILE OR IMBECILE

Communal disharmony & violence
Is certainly for most a bane
For peace loving people
For 'The normal' and 'The sane'
Peace and harmony gets disrupted
None of the communities gain

There is loss of personal property
There is loss of invaluable life
Fear is the obvious byproduct
Creating strain, stress and strife
Years of efforts and achievements gutted
Like, butter pierced with a hot knife

Infrastructure is ravaged
Which any nation can ill afford
Fear rules ordinary lives
Cause 'Seeds of hatred' are sowed
Lifestyles shattered, paupers overnight
Where once prosperity & harmony flowed

'Professional death dealers' start the fire
That the existing harmony maims
Destructive chain reaction follows
Each community the other blames
'Obsessed with sale' the media gathers rumours
While they gleefully 'Fan the flames'

Suprio Ghosh

Who pays the professionals?
To commit, 'Such insane deed'
Who benefits from this chaos?
And 'The hatred' and 'Fear', they breed
Investigative journalism
Is, what we urgently need

Mature, impartial, responsible
Ought to be, the media of today
To imbibe awareness
And show the ignorant, 'The way'
To heal national wounds
And transform, 'The reality of the day'

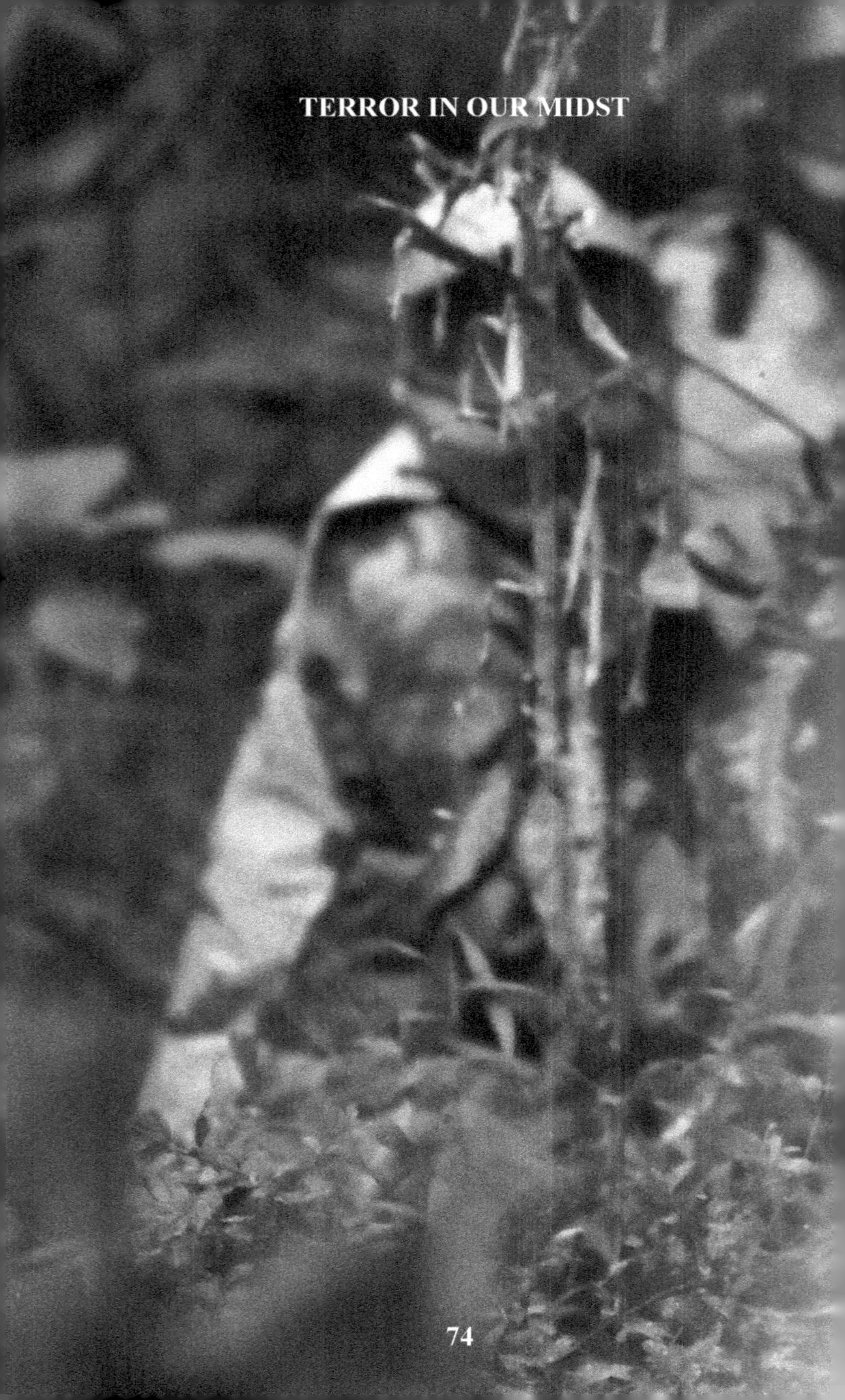

18. THE MUDDLED EAST 1.

The men clean their weapons
While the women silently weep
No one dares to oppose the elders
They need home, hearth and sleep

They need to live their daily lives
Their elders they dare not oppose
Who, align with powerful war-lords
And their insane dictates impose

Squandering away many lives
Sometimes a generation or more
Destroying reality through propaganda
To justify and to lure

Cannon fodder they require
While they for supremacy strive
They use their own ruthlessly
To keep their mischievous cause alive

To sacrifice oneself is holy
They seem to have convinced their lot
While keeping a major share
Of the booty the war lord had brought

Hatred they sprout
While religion they teach
Misinterpreting the sacred text
'Kill all non believers' they preach

Suprio Ghosh

Hate is profitable business
They, for sure, know
They misinterpret and mislead
While their coffers & glory grow

Suprio Ghosh

19. TERROR IN OUR MIDST 2.

Hark! The terrorist
Strikes once again
At will he strikes
Causing destruction & mayhem
Brainwashed by vested interests
He plays this vicious game

His rationality is warped
His mind, sharp but lame
Not realizing that he's a pawn
He plays this insane game
Not caring for life
He commits heinous sins without shame

The unholy warriors
Seek soft targets
They target the innocent
Without any regrets
A black mark on civilized societies
They're terrifying destructive pests

Motivated by warped ideology
The suicide bomber acts
He feels he is right
Though he's ignorant of the facts
May God give him sanity?
So that he retracts

TERROR IN OUR MIDST

The security forces
Are alarmed and piqued
The situation is deteriorating
Even though the security is pepped
Trying to spot terrorists among civilians
Leaves them perplexed and peeved

The ordinary shopkeepers & buyers
On any ordinary street
Are the ones who are killed?
Or maimed ends meet
Fear rules their lives
They trudge on, with trembling feet

The ordinary citizen
Live in constant fear
Everything becomes uncertain
Life to them, is dear
Helpless against such odds
Silently all stress they bear

The terrorist maims and kills
And causes tremendous pain
With dedicated actions he throws
Life & progress down the drain
One often wonders
Who from these mad actions gain?

How do they benefit?
From mayhem and pain
When they destroy, harmony, serenity
How can they gain?
Played by powerful warlords
They certainly couldn't be sane

Suprio Ghosh

Who finances such insane acts?
Who from this madness gain?
Maniacal minds initiate & perpetuate such strategy
Even though it's in vain
Society cannot be overwhelmed
With a dose of terror and pain

The tentacles of terror
Have spread far and wide
From 'The red army', 'Badermeinhof'
To PWG & Karenkaren who in jungles hide
There are many like LET and Al-Qaida
Who, were Osama Bin Laden's pride

Till sometime back
The epicentre was Afghanistan
Now it's shifted to its mother
The ISI and Pakistan
The tentacles are spreading
Wherever they can

They have spread around the world
To be precise
To lick their wounds
And reorganize
To replenish their armoury
With many a lethal device

We cannot afford to slip back
Into a barbaric & primitive cocoon
This menace of terrorism
Has to be eradicated soon
It will certainly be
For one and all a boon

Suprio Ghosh

So let us all unite
All people, all nations
Let's all work together
It'll be good for all nations
Peace & prosperity shall rule the day
For all people and all nations

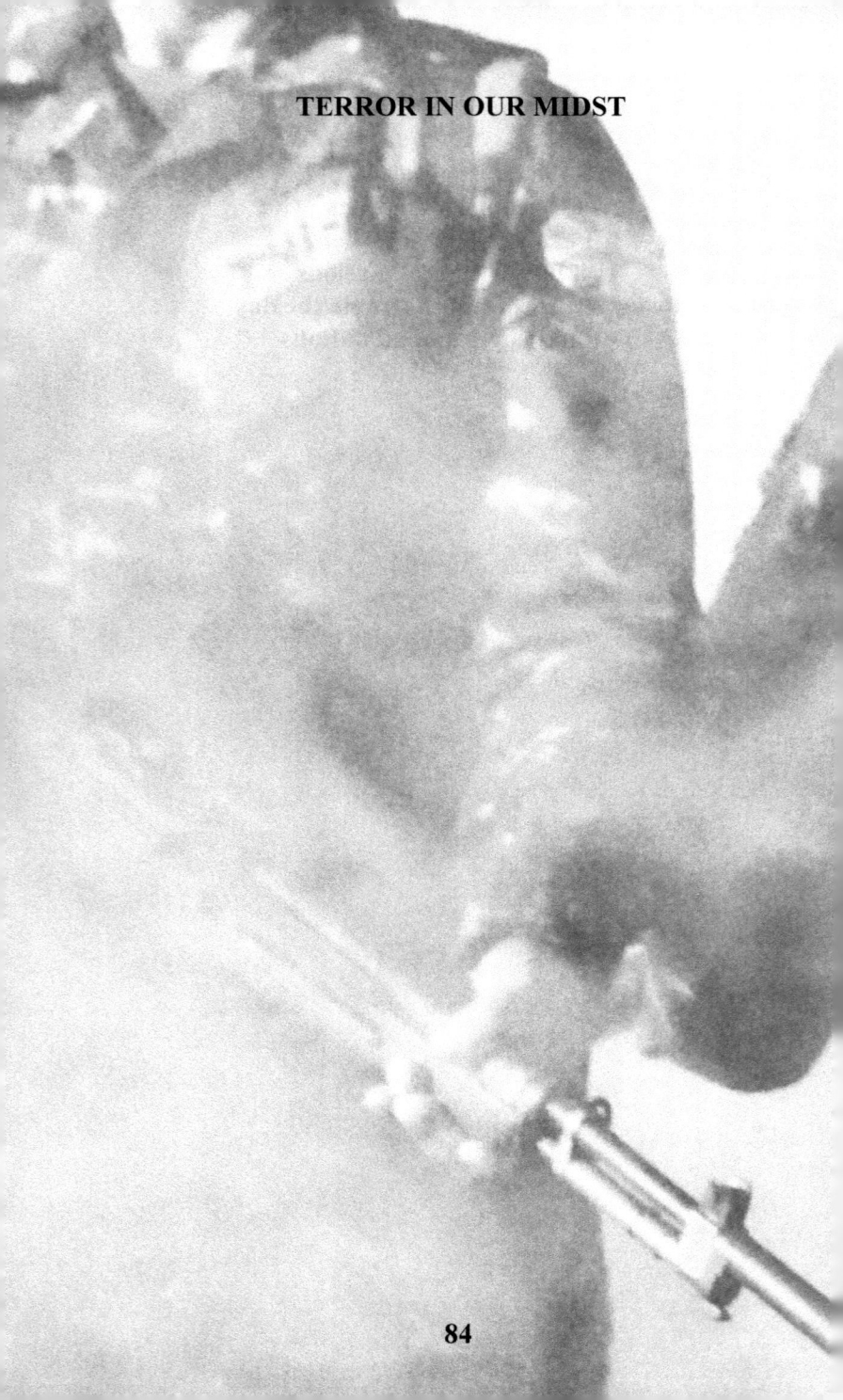

20. THE TERRORISTS

The terrorists exploded
An improvised device today
In the heart of the market
Not very far away
Bright sparkling colours
Became, vicious black and grey

The blast was of such intensity
Its impact one couldn't ignore
It killed many people
It maimed many more
It had the vicious power
To destroy & annihilate by the score

It disrupted many lifestyles and more
Many families, their stability
Their financial state of affair
Their harmony and cooperative ability
Problems associated with insane acts
The byproduct of senility

Maimed members and hospital bills
Which families could ill afford
Having lost breadwinners
For some, the end of the road
Life had always been tough, but happy
Now agony and another load

Suprio Ghosh

For the widow
Who will pay the food bill?
For the child
Who will eventually grind in a mill
And for the ones who govern
It's a vicious war and it's up hill

The terrorists strike with power & fury
What do they eventually gain?
They are merchants of misery
And harbingers of pain
Mad ideologues fuel their brain
Acts associated with the vicious & the inane

Breeding violence
Death destruction & pain
Terrorizing the public
Their acts inhuman, irrational and insane
The idiotic and selfish media
Supports and promotes this game

Of the mad ideologist
With a wicked mind
Senile, insane & wicked
Selfish, horrid & unkind
Defeating such evil is a must
Let's get together and a solution find

Suprio Ghosh

21. TERRORISM TODAY

Gaining footholds
Everywhere
Spreading tentacles
Here and there
They seem to be
Everywhere

Spreading fear
Spreading pain
Insane agendas
Conceived by the inane
Society is jittery
That's what they gain

To rule
By the power of fear, strictly
To rule
By the power of deception, silently
They spread the message
Blatantly, brazenly

They kill
Destroy & maim
They seek soft targets
Without shame
Do they really gain?
What a shame

They wish to conquer
By spreading fear
They've started giving dictates

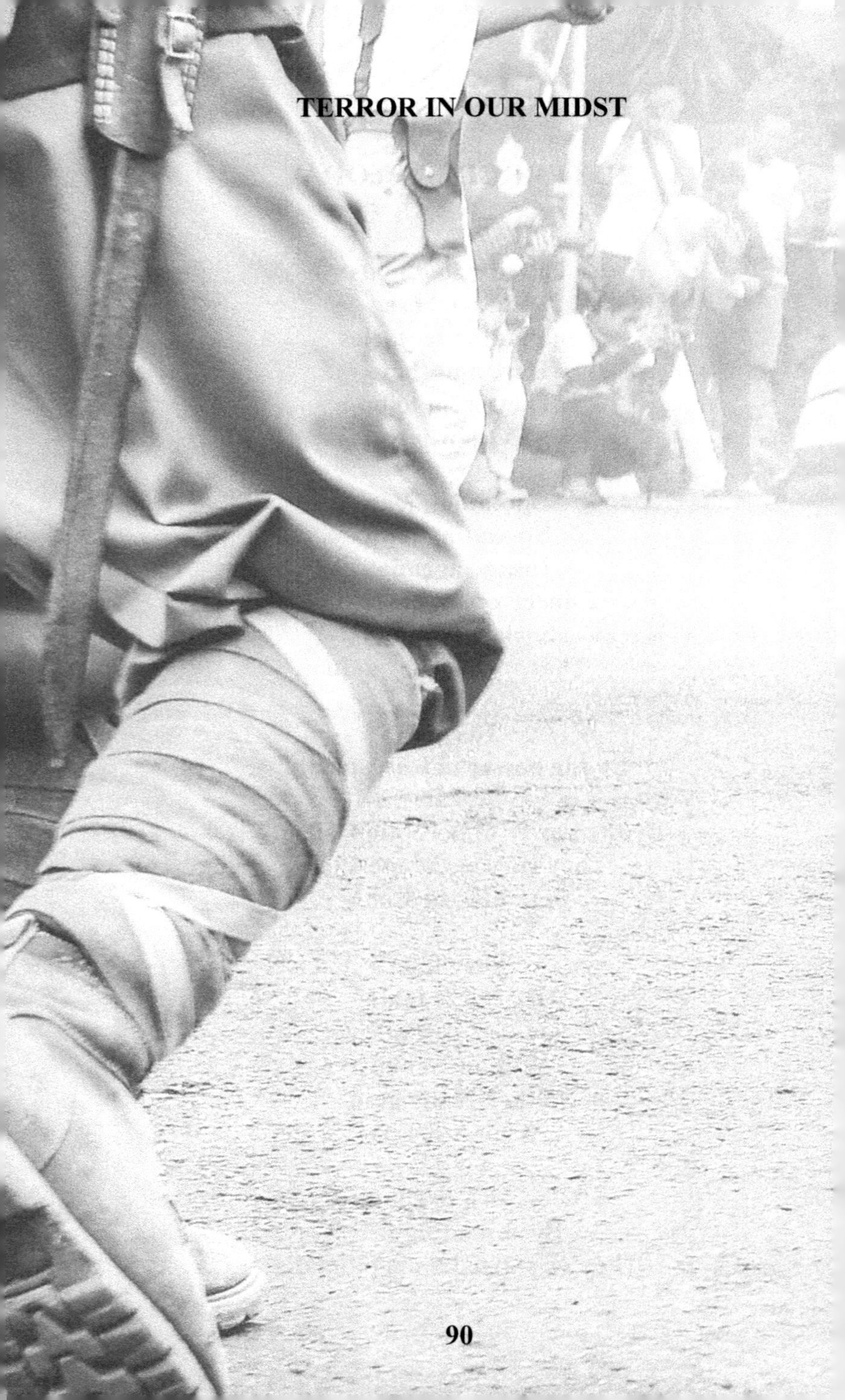

Suprio Ghosh

On an insane path they steer
Our reactions, usually disorganized & ineffective
Cause of disastrous policies & substandard gear

A primitive reality
They try to boost
Where primitive laws
Rule the roost
Barbaric laws
They try to boost

They are afraid of women
So they push them down
They're afraid of freedom
At it they frown
They're afraid of the rational, the sane & the just
They blast them out of town

To a distorted version of God
They bow to everyday
They are zombies of the warlords
It seems, they are here to stay
We must get rid of them
I'm sure there must be some way

There's still time
Let's try again
There's still a chance
To get rid of this pain
If all nations unite & try
We have plenty to gain

Suprio Ghosh

22. WHO WILL BELL THE CAT???

All nation of this world unite& cooperate
We have a war at hand
Strange evil beings are taking over
They come from every land

These evil beings are uniting
To take over and rule Planet Earth
Let us stop and eradicate this evil
If we understand sanity and freedoms worth

They have made their own country
And are expanding at a lighting pace
They don't care for international boundaries
Minorities in their land have no place

Let's stop them now
Before they soon be
Larger, more wicked and more barbaric
Ihope we don't have such days, to see

Some nations are war weary
They don't want to commit all their own
It's fair if they ask others to commit ground forces
Air power can't win this war alone

Why do nations keep professional armies?
If they are so afraid to fight
They should all join the coalition
And fight with all their might

Suprio Ghosh

Sophisticated ammunition and weapons
Who manufactures and supplies the terrorists?
What supply routes do they take?
Seems to be the work of a perfectionist

Or is it that we have traitors?
Here among our own
Who do anything to make money?
Even back-knife their own

The security agencies have a notion
Who breeds, feeds & nurtures this evil
That's expanding and establishing itself at a lighting pace
To destroy everything sane & civil

All nations must join hands
If we want to destroy this evil
If we want to save tolerance, freedom, equality, love
Peace, happiness, tranquillity & everything sane & civil

We can eradicate them
The future tells me that
With all our willingness and might
We together shall 'Bell the cat'
We together shall 'Bell the cat'
We together shall fight
Not with token assistance and words
But, with all our intelligence & might

But we must deactivate
Their supporters their recruiters & their suppliers first
To negate their capabilities
And put an end to their evil thirst

Suprio Ghosh

23. AWAKEN OH! MEDIA

Terror in our midst
Breeding fear each day
The media splashes gory details
With shocking news they make hay
Not caring about the minds they maim
For a bumper sale they pray

Many adults and youngsters
Find the violence attractive
Some align with the misconstrued cause
To play roles that are, active & passive
Instead of joining the mainstream
To lead normal lives, that are, constructive

The media helps the terrorists
Who need publicity for, their cause
Who need to know, various details
To plan the next strike without flaws
With enough brainwashed cadre & sponsors
To carry on without a pause

It lets them know
If their own managed to get away
About routes, they ought not, take
And safe houses, where they ought not, stay
About their ammo dumps that are confiscated
And the security strategy at play

Suprio Ghosh

About explosives that didn't function
Or when a strike fails
About nabbed militants who succumb to pressure
And expose many secret details
About the strength and deployment of the security
And many other important details

Shouldn't the media play?
A role, that is more mature
With information, disinformation and mind games
And to surrender, militants lure
With investigative journalism, exposing links to resources
To help, to eventually find a cure

Suprio Ghosh

24. I HOPE WE LEARN FROM THE PAST

The Mumbai carnage
Was a rotten shame
Shows how sloppy our security apparatus has been
How ineffective and lame

How our security agencies
Ignore vital facts
Info obtained through sacrifices & sweat
Unfortunately, there is none who reacts

Promises and pledges by politicians
To handle it better later
Political skills, for disaster management
To pacify with promises, a slimy vote bank baiter

Our security agencies ought to
Themselves, feel secure
Ought to feel the nation is with them
This confidence we must restore

One has seen many demos
Of the nation's functional inability
To provide proper & correct training
Modern weapons or appropriate facility

To have enough range
In their fire power
Appropriately clad, to feel safe
And go back home happily with a flower

Suprio Ghosh

We've a lack of a serious approach
Lack of slick coordination
We've a lack of info sharing policies
Slack & sloppy security of the nation

One has seen many demos
Of shortcomings in proper & correct investigate skills
One has seen many demos
Of outrageous policies and political overkills

Shows how our efficient fighting men
Are based far away and immobile
Shows how naïve our strategists usually are
How obsolete, unsound and facile

A viable strategy we must have
To neutralize the menace of terrorism
Sane education policies we lack
To eradicate this scourge, the menace of the terrorism

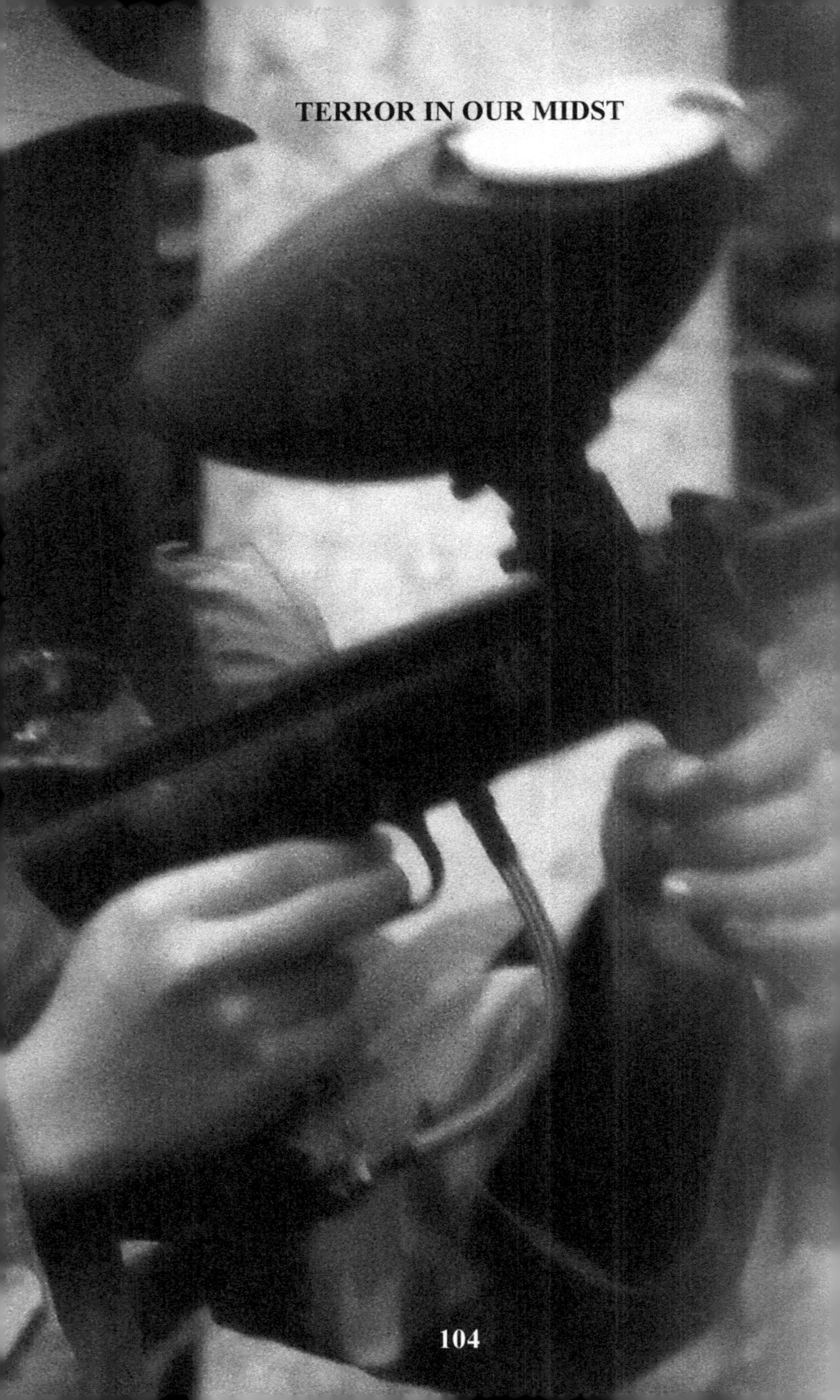

Suprio Ghosh

25. GROW UP

Spreading terrorism
Stability and serenity they rob
Thus fighting terrorism
Is every sane citizens job

No govt. can
Fight terrorism, on, it's own
Citizens must contribute
Weeding terrorism, wherever it's grown

They seek the unemployed & poverty ridden
To do their vicious & evil deeds
They buy them cheap to do their work
Their business and their needs

To dominate
Through violent acts
Manipulating minds
Manipulating facts

Destroying tolerance, creativity, progress
Peace, harmony & serenity of humanity
Sucking us back into barbaric times
Which mad ideologue teaches such insanity?

Which mad mind?
Plays this game
Egocentric & egomaniacal
Insane, inane, seeking power & fame

Suprio Ghosh

26. THINK ABOUT IT

Terrorizing soft targets
They gain cheap publicity
Financial benefits a part of the game
To overcome poverty and paucity

Terror by Islamic terrorists
Are more, in the news
Maybe, cause they are, so many
And try to impose their views

They are not the only terrorists
There are many more
Of different faiths, lands and hues
They are there by the score

Most are supported by powerful sponsors
From within their own land
Many receive support from foreign sponsors
Someone with a takeover plan

Where once there was
Love, peace, tolerance & harmony
Now madness is prevalent along with
Hate, horror, chaos & agony

Introspection & contemplation is the need
So that all nations can cooperate& unite
All terrorists we must neutralize
This barbaric evil we all must get together & fight

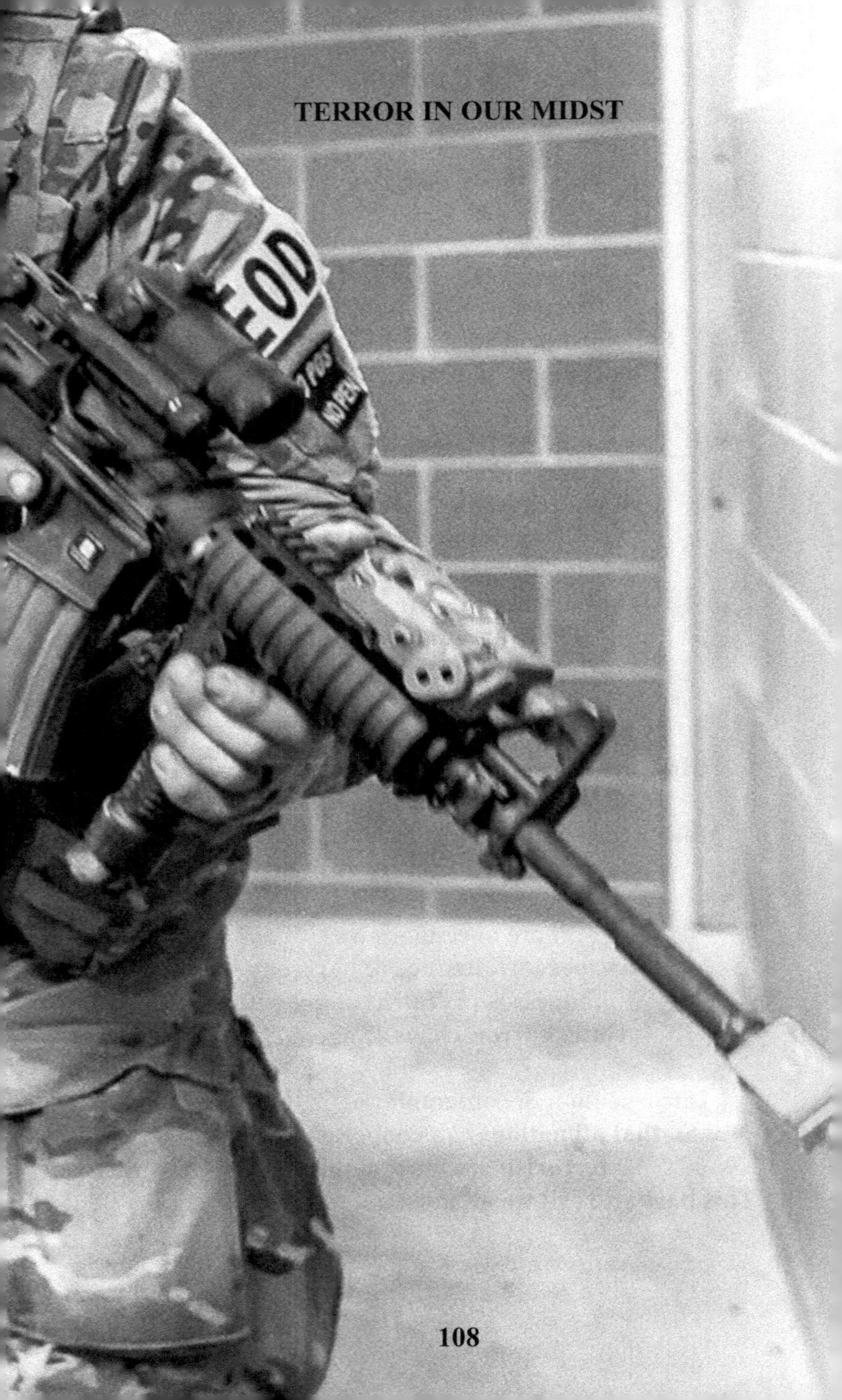
EOD

Suprio Ghosh

27. WHY???

Why, is one a terrorist?
Why does one terrorize?
What madness has taken over man?
What Insanity rules this vice?

Why does the media, give value to their cause?
Their deeds of barbarism & annihilation
Why not simply criticize their voice?
Their voice of death & destruction

Why not utilize investigative journalism
To expose the source of their resources
Why not utilize investigative journalism
To seek its root causes

What is the reason that they exist?
It, we must first eradicate
Why not heal if there is a way?
To cure and bring sanity to the day

What stops the media from?
Taking the sane way
What madness is 'Commercial success?'
That keeps insanity alive today.

TERROR IN OUR MIDST

28. IS THE MEDIA, HELPING THE
TERRORISTS???

The terrorists are spreading terror
Breeding fear each day
The media splashing avoidable details
With gory details they make hay
Till the public is blasted with avoidable news
They don't call it a day

For many average citizen
It is entertainment & attractive
Some align with the terrorists
Not understanding, the vicious and the negative
They too want to be, like the hordes in the news
And commit deeds which are lethal and destructive

They make money with
Irrelevant and avoidable news
Instead of using print space
For pleasant information or intelligent reviews
Or utilizing their influential power
For growth or any positive use

Terrorists cause mindless destruction
Cause mindless unacceptable pain
They strike fear in many hearts
The media promotes their game, to gain
Just to make a quick buck
They sensationalize the horrific & the insane.

Suprio Ghosh

29.TERRORISTS EXPLOIT COMMUNAL DISCORD, DISHARMONY AND TENSIONS

To gain footholds in any land
Giving away freebies & monetary donations
Always glib & with a forked-tongue
Loaded with negative motives & intentions

Money, weapons, ammunition
They give away for free
They build safe houses
And live in glee

They make friends who become
Over-ground ears and couriers
Transporting ammunition & food
And becoming false currency dealers

Since he's born, it's only poverty
Is, all he has ever seen
Suddenly a mountain of money
He's never had it so green

Not bothering about the consequences of crime
The consequences, associated hassles & more
They introduce their friends to the money pot
And there are safe houses by the score

The terrorists are well entrenched
Have safe houses, couriers, ammo dumps & more
They strike at will, anywhere & anytime
They're organized and this we can no longer ignore

Suprio Ghosh

Let us destroy them now
Before it's too late
Before their barbaric actions
Seal our fate

Suprio Ghosh

30. WHO ARE THEY?
WHO MAKE THE MOB???

Doesn't matter which class or ethnic stock
Ancestral descent, race, colour or breed
Love, peace, harmony and prosperity
Is in each one, an inborn need

The average Indian citizen
Have enough problems and woes
Socio-culture realities and endless bills
Keeps them on their toes

Children one must educate
Rent and associated bills to pay
Basic survival is an expensive game
They work at it, night and day

Keeping up with the Joneses'
Is not an easy game
Unpaid bills keep piling up
Every month it's the same

Regular inflation & skyrocketing costs
Makes it even worse
Helpless, they toil to keep ahead
Silently, they 'The system' curse
They have no mind or energy
They have no finance or time
For communal hatred & violence
Disharmony, turmoil or related crime

TERROR IN OUR MIDST

Who are they?
Who make the mob???
Obviously they're professionals & individuals in a frenzy
Who are picked to do the job?

Who pays them???
Who sponsors this mad show?
To divide us on communal lines
And seeds of hatred sow

Who manages the propaganda?
Who stores the petrol and arms?
That's so easily and readily available
That our harmony & prosperity harms

That bleeds the nation's
Meagre finance and resources
And deforms the mindset
Creating chain reacting 'Evil forces'

Do dubious politicians
Play 'This insane game'
Or do they, like ghouls
Benefit from 'This shame'
Like the 'Immature media'
That thrives on 'Controversial & shocking news'
Not bothering to investigate
Or print mature & sane views

Or is it 'The enemy'
From a land far away
Who fear our prosperity & progress?
Cause then they'll have 'No say'

Suprio Ghosh

True, it could be 'The enemy'
Who plan & sponsor this 'Insane show'
But it's the sons of our soil
Who, make the mare, go

For a pittance of personal gain
'Their souls' they have sold
They are professional 'Death dealers'
Political support makes them bold

Oh Lord! I can handle my enemy
But please save me from my own
Please help us to build sane citizen
And rectify where the weed has grown

We need a moderate mindset
Liberal in every way
One needs to mind one's own affairs
To 'Bring in', a progressive sway.

Suprio Ghosh

31. THE MAD MOTHER MIND

A powerful mad mind
Dedicated to evil
Who, impose his dictates
Doesn't care for what is civil

Doesn't care for what is civil
Doesn't care for the civilized
That man is a civilized social being
Never, understood or realized

Is it an isolated one or a club of many?
Who, have started pooling in resources
To fight and paralyze legal governments
And defeat & annihilate all legal forces

A mad mother mind
Is taking form
A mad mother mind
Dictates a new norm

It's taking form
The process of being born
Organizing and cultivating each evil skill
Viewing the civil & the civilized with scorn

Bringing with her
A barbaric turbulent storm
A crystal clear display
Of mans most hideous form

Suprio Ghosh

A powerful mad mind
Categorizing, organizing
Each skill of annihilating
Each skill of terrorizing

A mad mother mind
That dwells on evil
An insane mother mind
That ignores and degrades anything civil

The byproduct
Hell on earth
The losses
Everything that has worth

Unity & cooperation among all nations
Is, the first need of the day
Only then can the civilized have
The correct strategy to win the day

To get rid of this evil forever
All sane people, unite now
All nations unite now
To squash this evil somehow

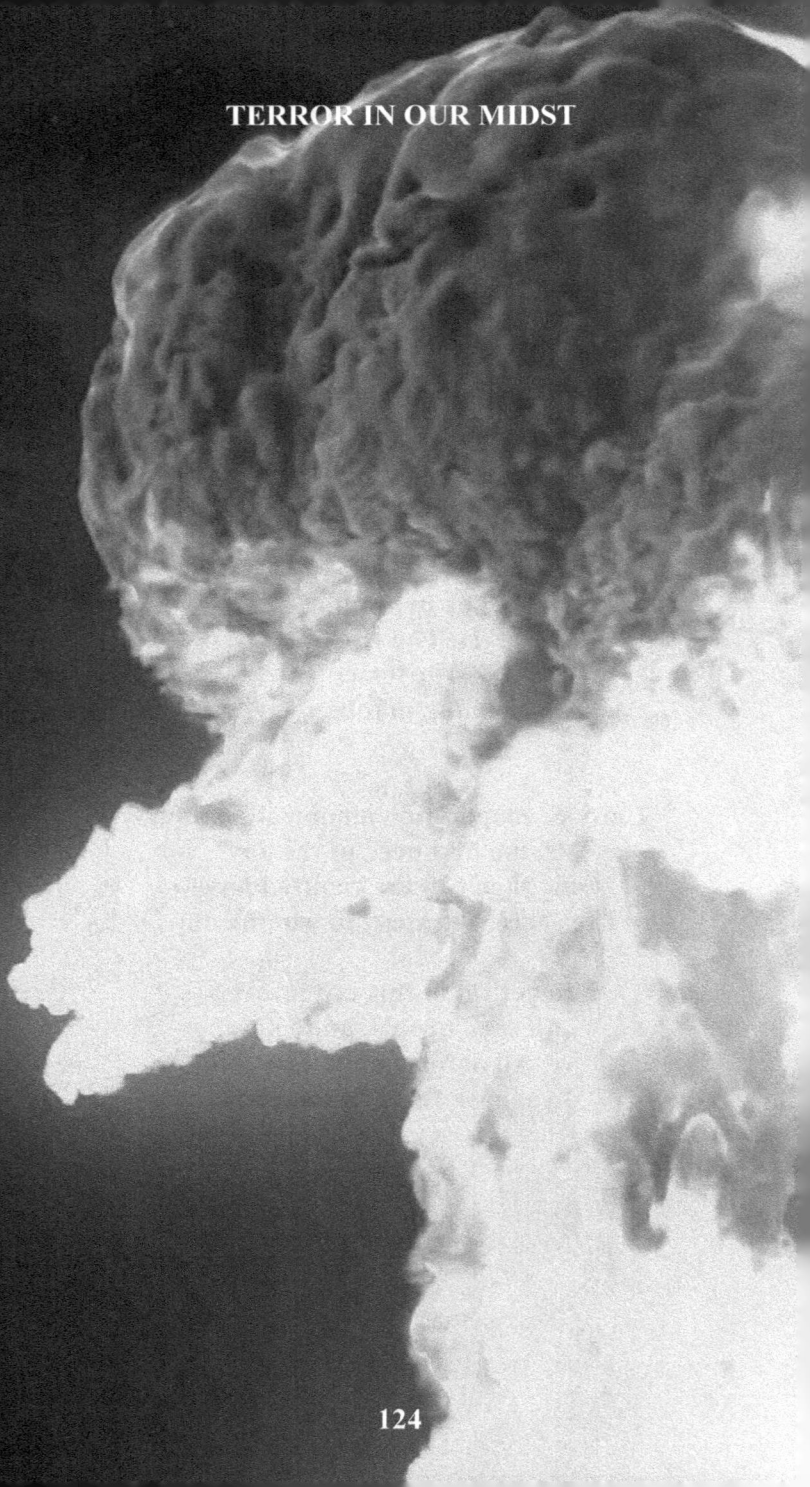

Suprio Ghosh

32. MEANINGLESS TREATIES

Mad men, playing mad games
To divide and rule
Manipulating, through religious sentiments
The ignorant public they fool

The media caters to
Their need to spread their voice
The fourth estate, irresponsible and immature
Sensational news for a quick buck, is their choice

Instead of giving a helping hand
To crush the terror machine
The media cashes in
On, the horrific & the mean

Investigative journalism
Is, the need of the day
To keep Terrorism
In its totality at bay

Cause its tentacles are
Many and very mean
Nothing so horrific
One has ever heard of, or seen

It's breeding poison, horror
In various unheard of forms
Destroying our reality, our abilities
Civilized processes, civilized norms

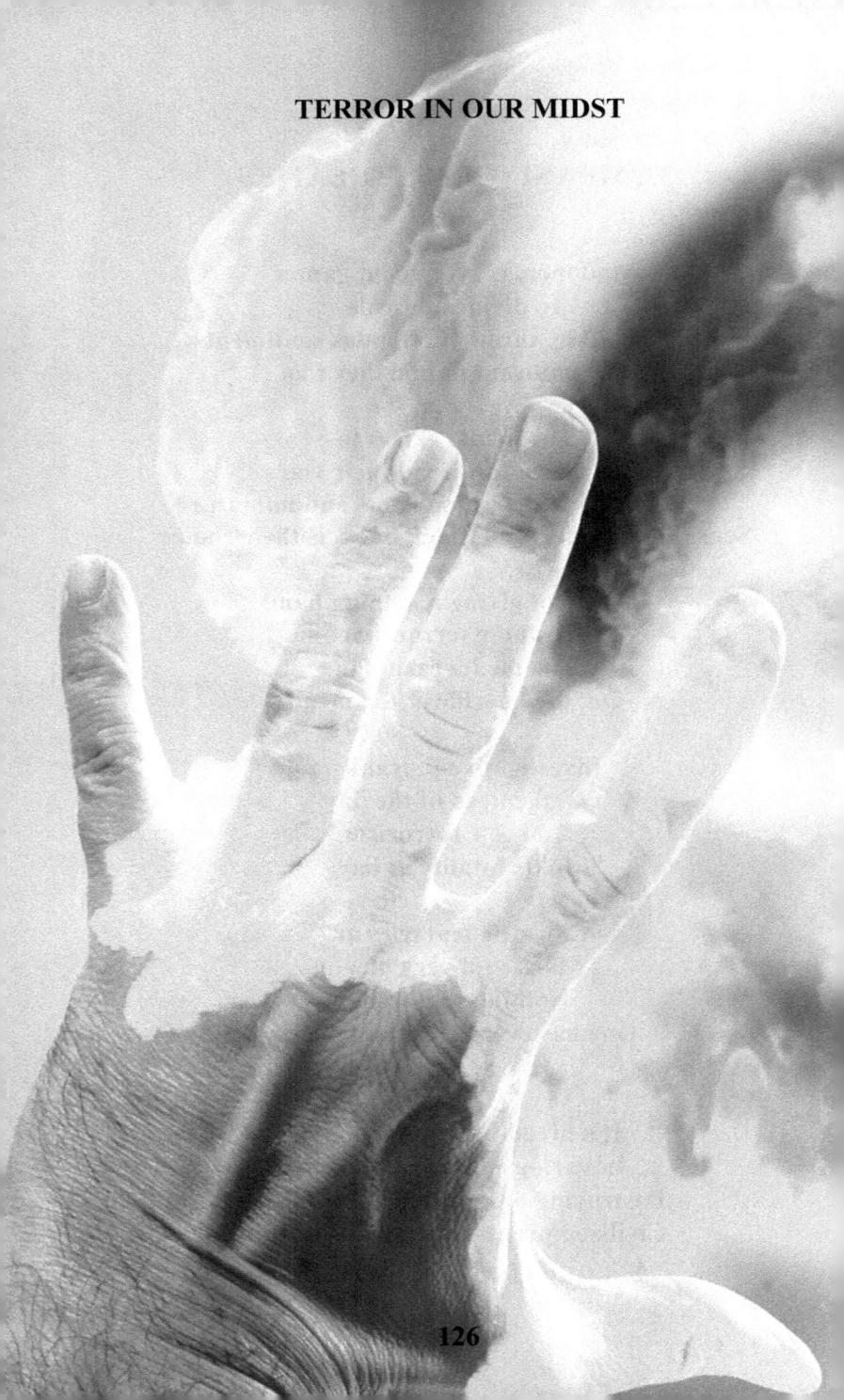

Suprio Ghosh

The terror machine is working overtime
Destroying lives, lifestyle, spreading pain
Destroying infrastructure, stability & harmony
Does anyone really, from such madness gain?

Its footholds are stronger
The monster has grown
It has started dictating terms
And making its presence known

We are proposing peace initiatives locally
Have we become incapacitated or mad?
Or have we, run out of strategies to win this war
It's really bad and very sad

Peace treaties with mad men
Have no meaning at all
Crush them in a united manner
Otherwise, in time we may fall

Of course everybody
Deserves a second chance
But do wicked men
Keep, their word and stance

I pray to God
That, things gets better
If not right now
Sooner or later

Suprio Ghosh

33. WAKE UP All NATIONS

Professional is the Caliph's brainwashing technique
It makes sane people evil and mad
The slaves comply willingly
They are only too happy and glad
What's happening to our world???
This is truly very sad

This cruel breed
We must eradicate
This, we must achieve
There is a lot at stake
Let's wake up to this reality
And sane decisions & actions make

Let's make sane decisions
Let's do it right
With an invisible & lethal enemy
We are in the middle of a fight
May, all nations cooperate
And fight with all their might

TERROR IN OUR MIDST

34. PLEASE LISTEN ALL NATIONS

Sunnis of a different kind
They are even slaughtering their own
They are slaughtering here and there
Their evil powers have grown
Madness of this kind
This world has never known

Seeds of sadness & sorrow were sown
The day this evil was born
Serenity, tranquillity, peace, love
Freedom and sanity were all torn
The choice to live how one chooses
Was dead and gone

The   monster has become very large
And many tentacles it has grown
Each more cruel and barbaric than the other
The seeds of doom till now unknown
No respectfor the law, national borders, and cultures
The consequences are well known

If wedon't catchtheir supporters & suppliers immediately
It might become too late
Then only the future knows
What will be our fate?
Lightning quick they expand their domain
It's at an unbelievable rate

Suprio Ghosh

Stop them now
If you dare
Stop them now
If you care
Stop them now
For your family welfare

Unity among all nations
Is the urgent need
Not just words or token assistance
With all their might, is the need
This has to be done now and immediately
It is the urgent need

TERROR IN OUR MIDST

Suprio Ghosh

35. IT'S TIME TO PONDER

They hide behind deceptive covers
They strike to destroy and kill
They strike to create mayhem and terror
They strike at will

They communicate through the media
Giving dictates to any republic
Gory details and visuals are published
Terrorizing the general public

It's only through the media
Their deeds are highlighted
Using the media as an info bank
Their plans are farsighted

They are out to destroy
Peace and harmony
They want chaos to reign
Not tolerance in symphony

They come from different societies
Giving their own a bad name
It's only because of media coverage
They become pawns, in this game

With only financial gains in sight
The media flashes shocking news
Fanning the flames without a thought about the cure
Thus the terrorized public has confused opinions & views

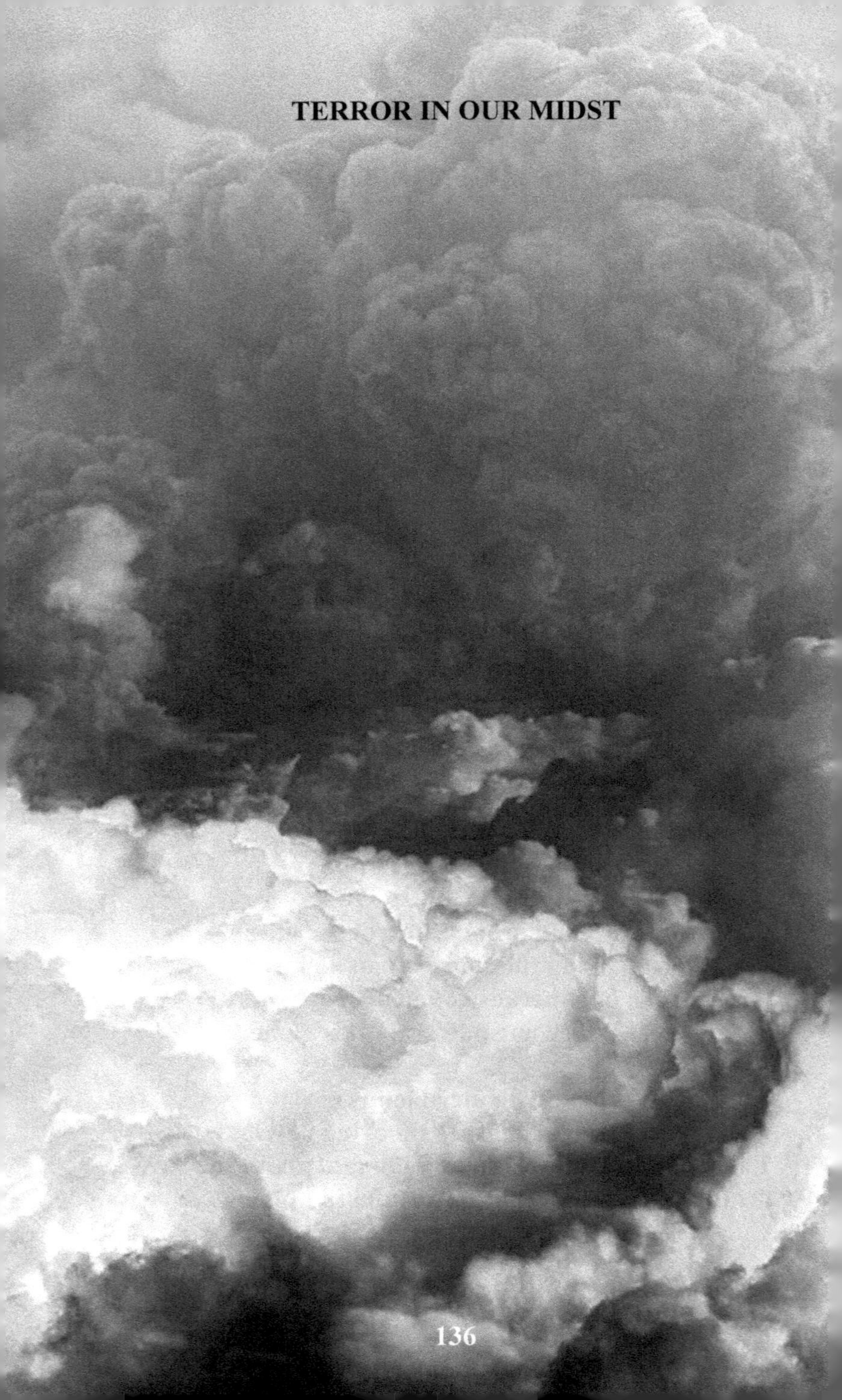

Suprio Ghosh

It's time to make new laws
The media we must constrain
It strengthens the cause of the terrorists
Who many footholds from it gain

It's time the media realized
That it's a complex battle we fight
We all have the responsibility to contribute
Towards victory and the might of right

36. ERADICATING EVIL 'IS'

Battle hardened   warriors
Became mercenaries for sale
Doing their new masters bidding
Spreading cruelty & pain without fail
Their master's brain-washing techniques
Is creating a blood-thirsty trail

Cruelty is their trade mark
Barbarism is their sense of joy
Brutality is their new profession
Imposing their ideology is the ploy
Don't we understand this?
Are we either imbeciles or coy?

Mass executions is their norm
Beheading a weekly affair
Their routine insane actions
Certainly creates a scare
How do we eradicate this evil?
Is there no one there?

Some nations are trying
Some giving token assistance
This is a miniscule of what ought to be done
To destroy their tough resistance
All nations ought to contribute with all their might
The civilized require more assistance

Suprio Ghosh

What is the solution?
How do we eradicate this evil?
That tries to destroy
Everything sane and civil
Blitzkrieg their technique to take over the world
And impose new laws, norms and sanity level

The only solution is
All nations must unite
Not with token assistance
But with all their intelligence & might
Let us realize this reality
We have a tough war to fight

Suprio Ghosh

37. TWO POWERFUL TENTACLES OF TERROR

Two tentacles of the terror machine
Have become very powerful & gigantic
Eradicating the IS or Boko haram
Is not going to be a very easy trick

Eradicating their leaders will not help
Cause new ones will take their place
What's amazing is that of their financers
There is absolutely not a credible trace

From where and how their food
Medicines ammo & more come
And who pays for
This astronomically massive sum

It takes convoys of loaded trucks
To fulfil their daily needs
What invisible routes do they take?
Or is it that no one heeds?

Their recruiting and brain washing techniques
Are very convincing and successful
They turn normal beings into barbaric zombies
Their techniques are certainly powerful

Where are the stores
That stock, such massive quantities
What distribution systems do they apply
No dearth of commodities

Suprio Ghosh

Their training camps are never detected
As though they are in some foreign soil
Their training methodology truly amazing
Teaching sane people to create turmoil

Teaching sane people to be brutal
To be barbaric, beastly & evil
Teaching, that it's not worth it
To be normal, kind and civil

Teaching , that it's not worth it
If they don't fight for 'Their cause'
Teaching that, so what if they die
They ought to fight on without a pause

Their Blitzkrieg techniques are successful
They are expanding at an alarming pace
Their deceptive ways are very calculative
Of their leaders there is no trace

It's a pity if we become their slaves
And have to face their ways
It's a pity if we have to face their brutality
I hope we never see such days

If we don't eradicate them now
Maybe we never ever can
If all nations cooperate and fight
We shall and we can

Suprio Ghosh

38. THEY HURT THEIR OWN

'God is great',they yell
While committing an evil deed
Their propaganda with religious overtones
Gives a bad name to their creed
Terrorize ruthlessly,a self imposed agenda
Seems to be their need

Destroying families,harmonious lives
Common citizen who don't understand it all
Destroying infrastructure,causing inconvenience
What do they try to stall?
Destroying harmony&religious tolerance
Is secularism heading for a fall???

Members of their faith are looked upon
With suspicious and wary eyes
Biased behaviour,they face in society
While the law their privy pries
Shunned,as though a leper
Each sane member for interaction cries.

Suprio Ghosh

39. THE MUDDLED EAST 2.

Sunnis by birth
Killers by deed
Bringing a bad name to their own
What is the need???

Misinterpreting, to commit fraud
The words of their prophet and God
For personal glory and wealth
The insane are taking over Oh! Lord

The moderate don't seem to have a voice
They don't have, much of a choice
Fear dictates the path they tread
Sanity requires courage& to be in poise

Courage to speak out, what's right
Courage to stand up against evil and fight
So that sanity may survive
Courage to be a part of God's might

Suprio Ghosh

40. HAVE THE 'IS' LOST THE WAR???

The 'IS' have lost their territories
But is that the cure
More than half of their forces have escaped
Planning lethal attacks which we will have to endure

Suicide bombings & soft targets
A favorite with them
Whichever way possible
They try to cause death destruction & mayhem

They want us to be paranoid
So that they can rule the roost
With a sword in the hand that beheads
Their beliefs & norms they impose & boost

Our Global Village must get rid of such evil
But how can it be done?
If we don't nab their financers, recruiters & suppliers first
We can't decimate their 'Power of the gun'

Let's wake up to our reality
And do what ought to be done
If all nations join hands & cooperate
This war is as good as won

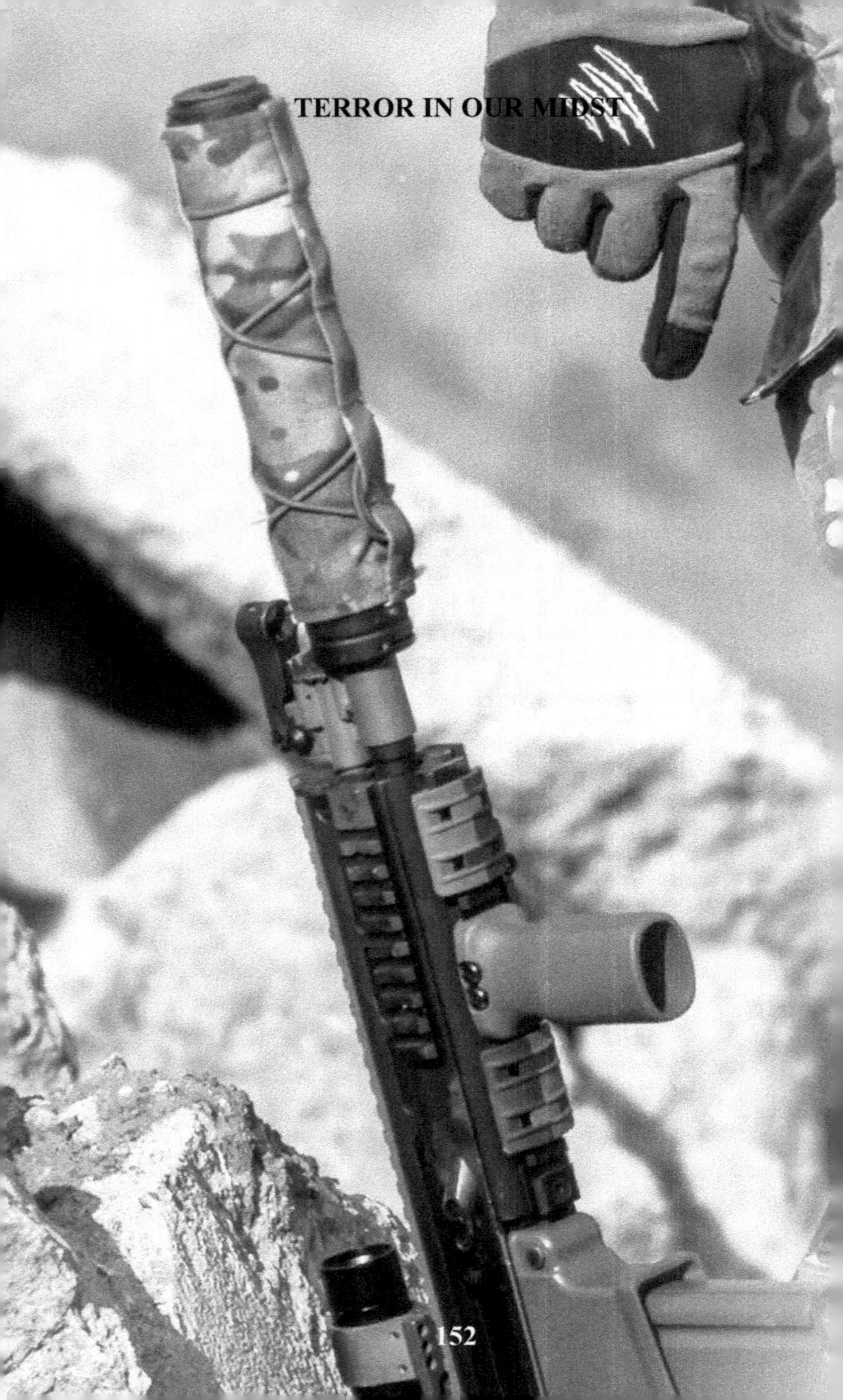

Suprio Ghosh

41. ANOTHER INVISIBLE ENEMY

The 'IS' have become an invisible enemy
Like the Al Qaeda and many more
They are always executing unpredictable lethal attacks
Something, for which we need a cure

Don't all nations understand?
It's cooperation among all nations we need
We need to share information & intelligence
If we want to defeat this strange breed

They have spread more or less all over the world
That's why all nations ought to unite
It is the only way
To win this fight

To nab their financers, recruiters
And more
Hitting them where it hurts
Is the cure

Decimating their power of the gun
Will put a dent on their might
Cooperation among all nations
Will help us win this fight

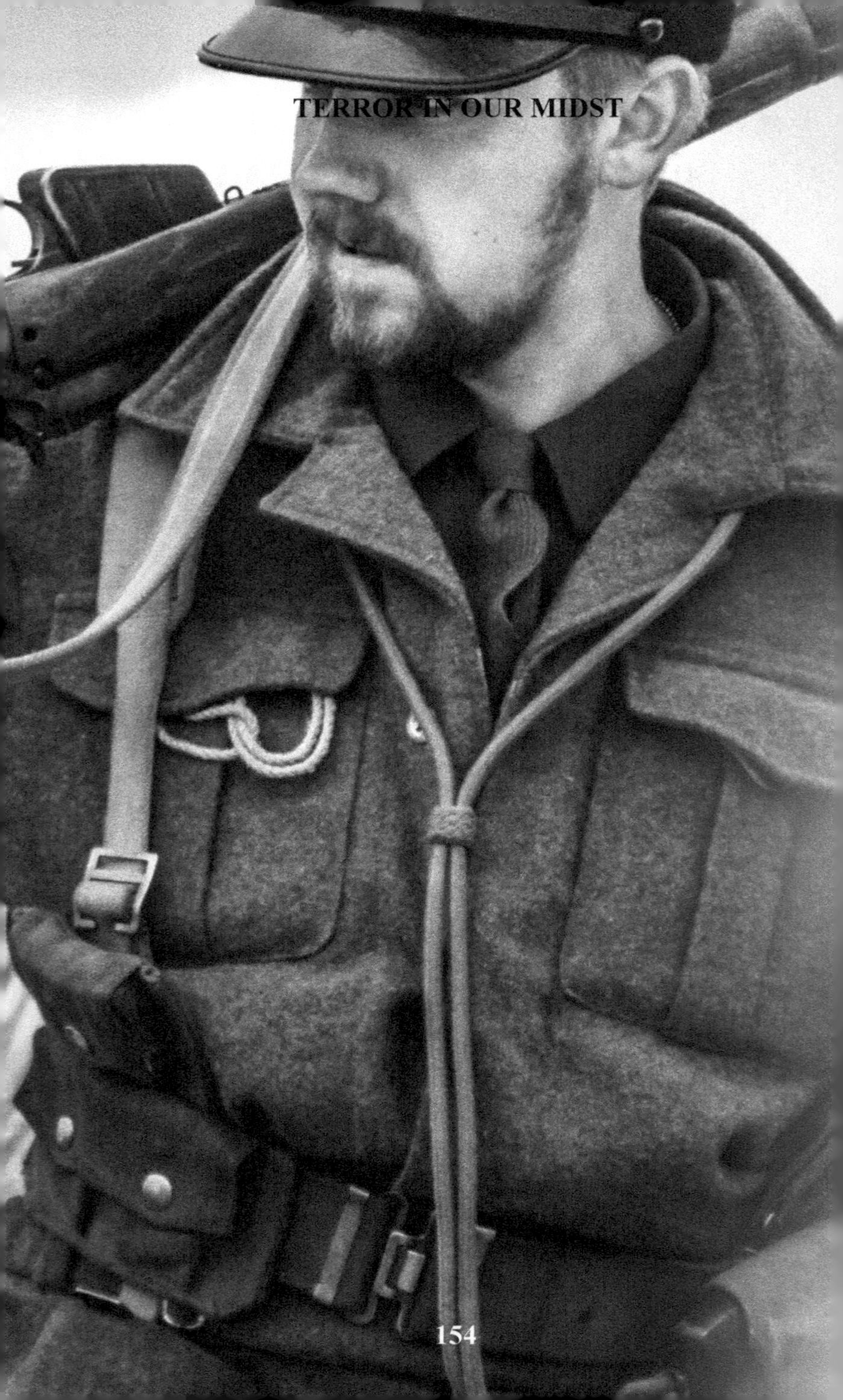

Suprio Ghosh

42. TOUGH ON TERRORISM

Being tough on terrorism
Is, the need of the day
Making and implementing tough laws
Is the only way

When will politicians understand?
Every citizen wants to be safe & secure
And stop indulging in vote bank politics
Or predictable disaster lure

We require political ideologues
Whose first priority, 'The people of the nation'
Who teach us to sacrifice for others?
Not just for the 'Parties' domination'

Not make moves or issue dictates
Only for political gains
Utilize politics as a development platform
And not play idiotic domination games

Work for communal harmony
Not divide society on communal lines
Not breed hatred, acrimony, violence
Cause the nation then heads for chaotic times

Mayhem & horror
Due to political chimes
Is the nation disintegrating?
Harmony disappearing, due to gruesome crimes

TERROR IN OUR MIDST

Planned attacks on sleepy villages
Beheading man, woman and child
Wiping out communities in the name of God
Insanity, causing havoc, running wild

Like frogs who think their pond's the world
Contemporary political ideologues conceive & move
Destroying the nation, for whims & notions
One wonders what they are trying to prove

While ignoring international terrorism
And other manmade disaster calls
Fighting like cocks in a rooster pen
Making cracking ignominious & insane destructive calls

Terrorism is spreading at a high speed
But most governments are still soft on terror
Is our war against terrorism?
Being fought with callousness and error

We need a centralized command
To deal with this modern crime
We need to curb this monsters growth
While it is still in its prime

We need to overhaul
Our bureaucracy
No respect for our warriors
Is insulting and crazy

The media requires strict guidelines
We have a real proxy war on
Not sensationalize for gain, name, fame,
Not ruin strategies cause this war must be won

Suprio Ghosh

This war has to be won
To achieve peace, prosperity, progress& more
If we don't
'Hell on earth' is in store.

Suprio Ghosh

43. STILLTHERE IS TIME

Still there's time to unite & cooperate
To defeat the armies of terror
Still there's time to unite & cooperate
To defeat the sponsors of horror

Let's change traditional foreign policies
And cooperate to fight the armies of terror
If we don't do it now
We are committing a grave error

If they are not with us, they're against us
Is, a stupid way to think
Our Global Village is heading for disaster
We are on the brink

All nations ought to unite & cooperate
To fight and defeat the armies of terror
Let's do it right
And leave no room for error

44. BETTER POLICIES PLEASE

Those who terrorize us, are evil
Those who terrorize others, may be civil
This approach never works, let's seek a sane level

Condemn all of them
Isolate all of them
Brainwash all of them

Stop clandestine weapons & ammunition deliveries
Stop clandestine medical aid deliveries
Stop clandestine footstock deliveries

Stop using mercenaries for a good cause
Stop unaccountable ammunition production, without a pause
Stop repressive policies & correct the obvious flaws

45. UNITE & COOPERATE HONESTLY

With lethal weapons, they terrorize
The ordinary and the sane
Destroying lives, lifestyles & causing agony
What do they gain?
Faceless, Ruthless, with no dignity or shame
How? Why? Who caused this bane?

Extreme poverty
Discrimination & disparity
Leaves little room for sanity
Restructure society
Cooperate and save this world
Or else it is a shame on humanity

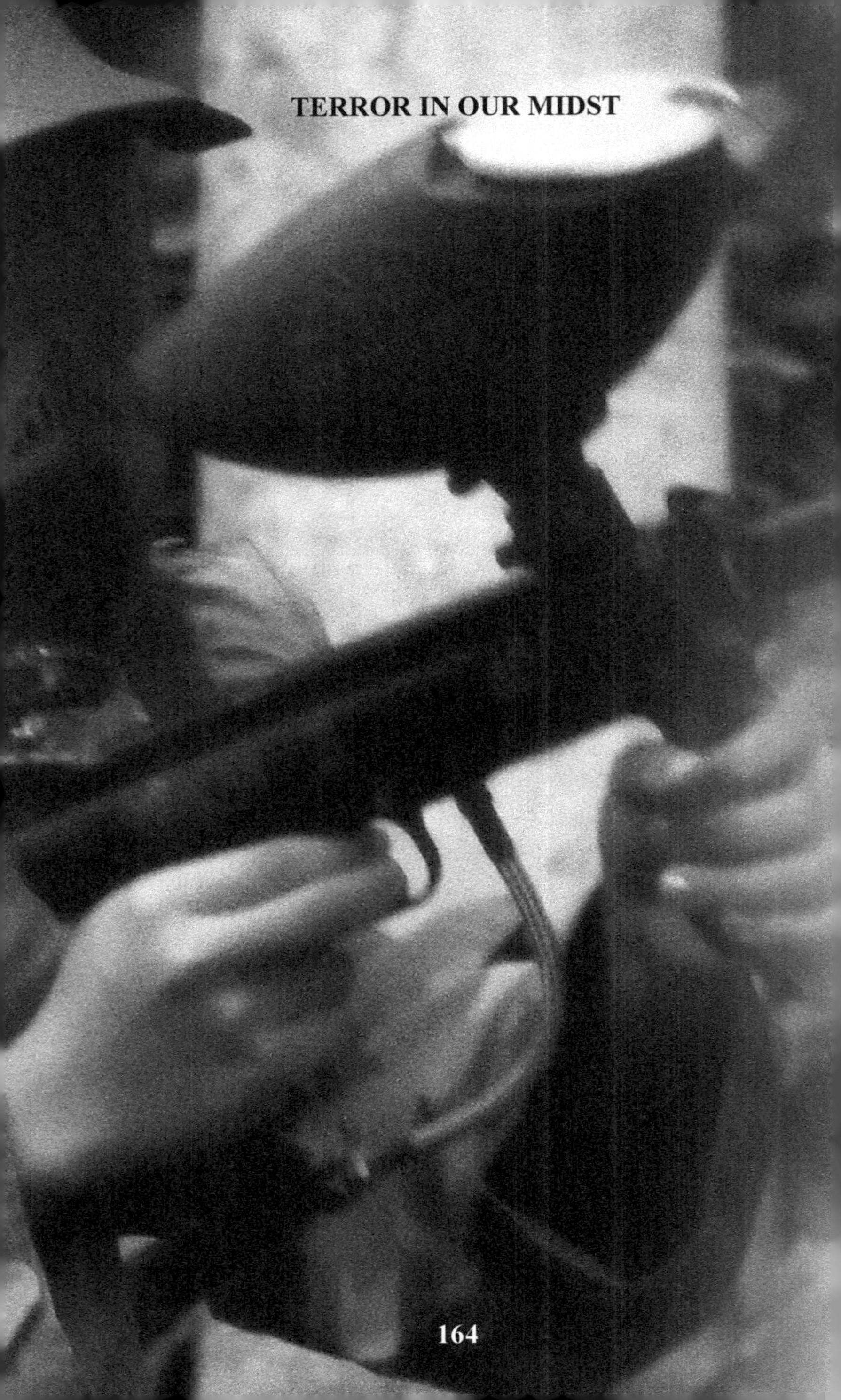

46. WE HAVE TO

Mad men are trying to take over the world
We have to do everything to stop them
They want to dictate terms & dominate
We have to do everything to stop them
They are inhuman, brutal & barbaric
We have to do everything to stop them

Suspicion looms in the air
We have to do everything to stop them
They have no respect for the sane & the civilized
We have to do everything to stop them
They have no respect for man, woman or child
We have to do everything to stop them
They have no respect for freedom & love
We have to do everything to stop them

Suprio Ghosh

47. TERROR IN OUR MIDST 3.

Terror in our midst
Insecurity in the mind
A reality of today
Its solution we must find

Cause it's a complex bundle
Of stubborn knots to untie
A horrific dangerous maze
For those who give it a try

For those who believe
In good overcoming evil
For those whose values are
Just, sane and civil

For those who through dialog
Find reasonable and just solutions
For those who prefer
To shun violence & hold negotiations

This horror was created
By some schools of thought
Who, perpetuate & nurture egomaniacal philosophies
It is 'Dictatorial power' they sought

Power they try to achieve
No matter which way
They believe, it's only they
Who ought to have a say

TERROR IN OUR MIDST

Their dictates ought to
Rule the rest
It's only they who deserve
The very best

They perpetuate fear
In many financial circles
To receive donations
Bucketfuls & not just trickles

Blackmail, extortions
To finance their agenda
Misinformation, disinformation
To spread their propaganda

They have more resources than governments
To finance their ghastly show
They have barbaric & viscous methods
They coax & manipulate to grow

Intimidating citizen through fear
Coaxing & cajoling for resources
They are usually better equipped
Than the law enforcing forces

They make use of our disunity
Our lack of harmony and greed
Don't we realize?
It helps terrorism breed

What's going on?
Something ought to be done
We ought to somehow, stop violence
Crush this 'Culture of the gun'

Suprio Ghosh

They equate themselves
To the messengers of the Gods
Quoting & misinterpreting to manipulate
To instigate pain, misery & frauds

They spread terror
To create fear in society
To make every citizen feel insecure
They destabilize in many a variety

So that their dictates
Are willingly obeyed
So that their philosophies
Are bowed to and prayed

48.WHO IS RESPONSIBLE?

Terrorist striking at will
Spreading fear and pain
Terrorizing with ruthless ferocity
Actions, of the insane

Terrorizing with ruthless tactics
The common citizen they hurt
The security people, always perplexed
No matter how alert

The security can't comprehend
How to control the situation
No proper equipment, data or strategy
To be able to, save the nation

Who is responsible?
For this lack of ability
How do we correct the situation?
And achieve stability

Achieve a sane policy
To have success
Achieve a sane path
To get out of this mess

Power they try to achieve
No matter which way
They believe, it's only they
Who ought to have a say

49. DEMOLISH THE TERROR MACHINE

The terror machine is winning
It's time to stop it, on its track
Still there is time to demolish it
But, it's unity that we lack

All nations must unite
In words and actions
Not follow traditional external policies
With knee jerked reactions

Our pain is pain
Their pain is O.K.
It's primitive thinking certainly
Senseless in the world of today

Financial wrangles to destabilize nations
Has become the cotemporary norm
Deceit, to achieve superiority
In every way or form

Hidden agendas, classified dictates
Diplomacy to achieve unofficial goals
No matter which way
Deceit, bribes, blackmail or doles

If we don't stop all this
Soon, it be the end
Cause the terror machine never will be
Or has been anybody's friend

Suprio Ghosh

Far and wide
Its tentacles have spread
Its madness and lethal power
We all know well and dread

We must get together to fight
The deadly terror infrastructure
It's already a bit late
Is a sane conjecture

They are not ours or theirs
They are all equally wicked & insane
Let's get together and grab their jugular
We all, have a lot to gain

Let's not support them
In covert or overt ways
If we can neutralize them
The world will see better days

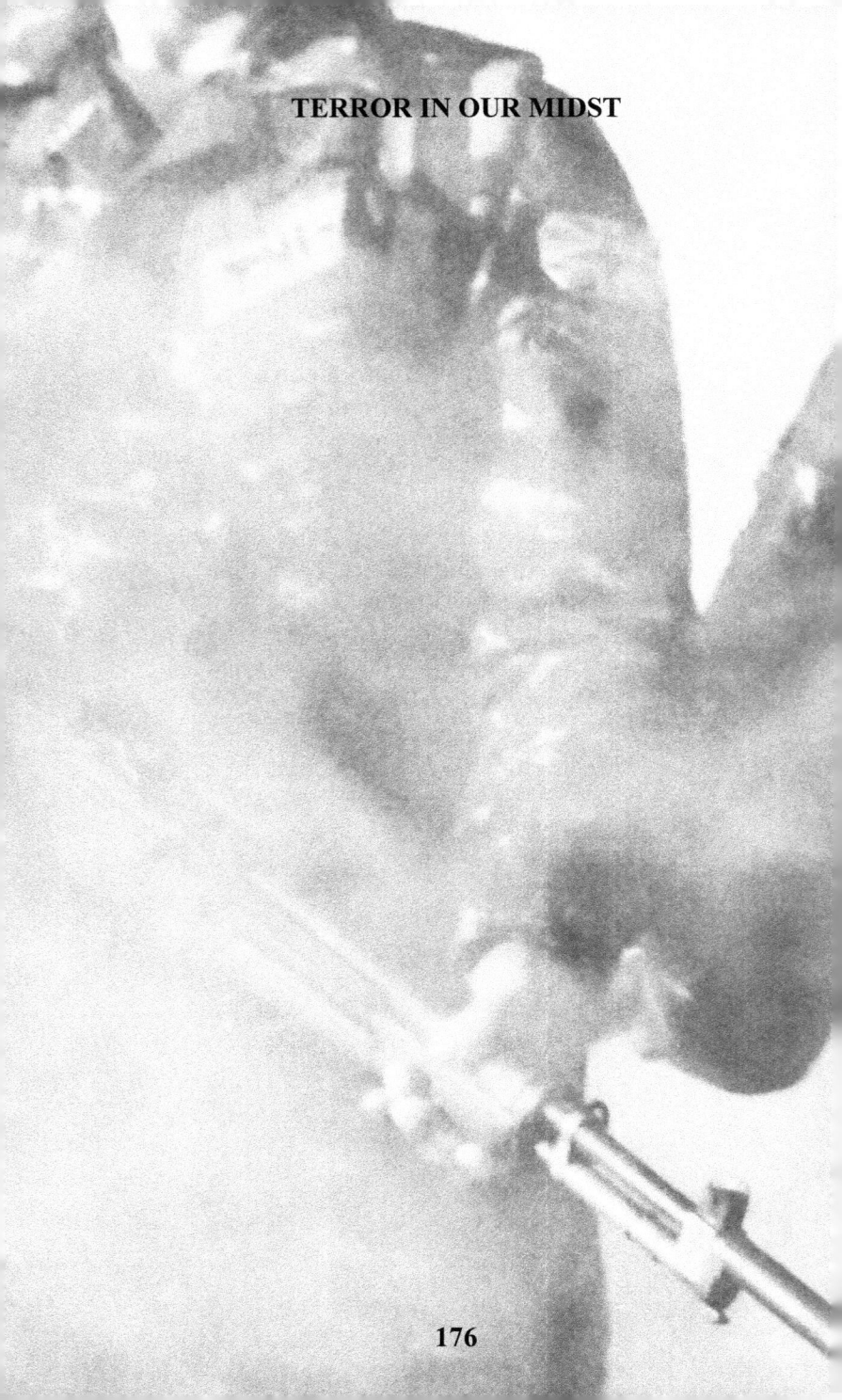

50. PLEASE REALIZE AND COOPERATE

We must exclude politics
From our war against terror
It's, a new dimension
It's a path, one ought not, tread with error

We must realize
That the terrorist has no religion
We must realize
That the terrorists belong to no region

He only uses them
To justify his cause
He slyly quotes & misinterprets
To destroy, without a pause

He misuses, to create terror
Of, many a horrific variety
He misuses to create chaos
In a sane and civil society

All nations must realize
That it's time to cooperate
Let's do the obvious, the sane
Before it's too late

The monster, though wounded
Is very much awake
Relocating, regrouping
Is for it, at stake

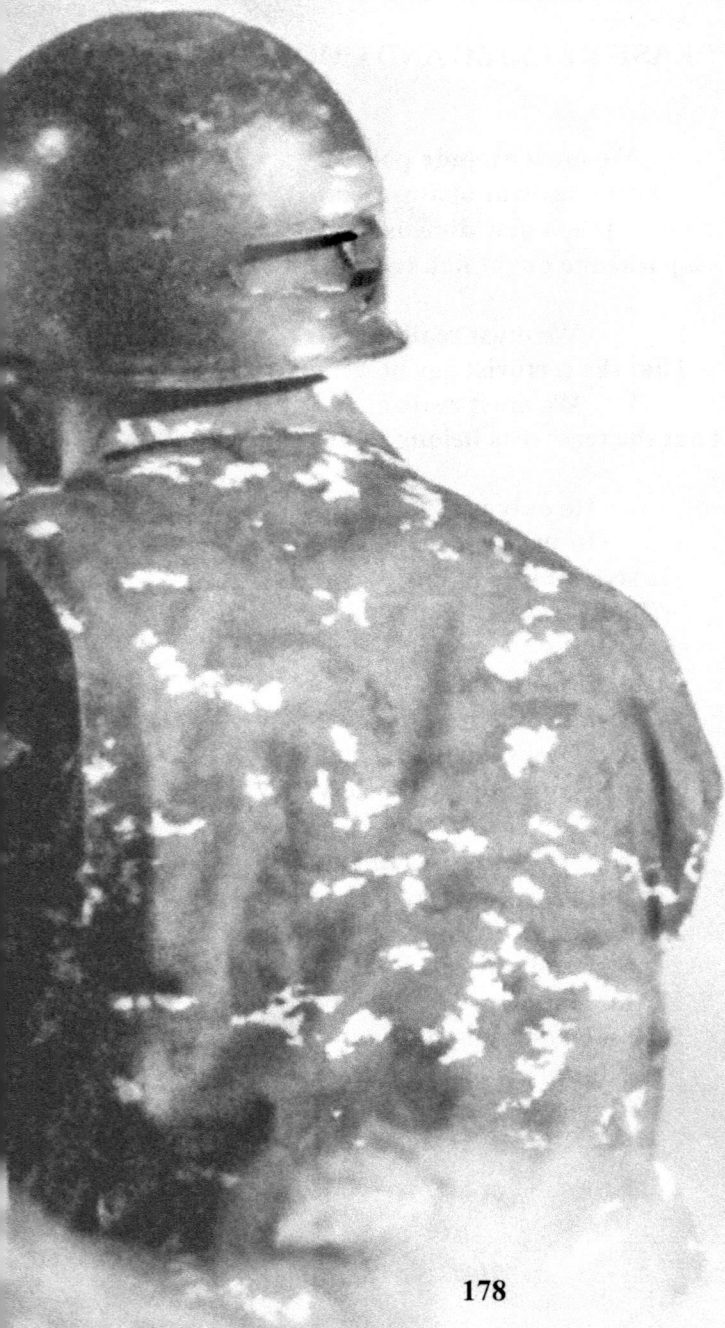

Suprio Ghosh

All nations of the world must work together
In this war against terrorism
While governments pay lip service, this monster grows
Waging war against freedom & secularism

All nations must cooperate
And pool in their resources
All nations must cooperate
To fight the evil forces

Evil forces that mire freedom, love, peace & happiness
Creating chaos to destroy
Tolerance, brotherhood, progress
Cooperation and joy

51. UPROOTING TERRORISM

Unity among all nations is the need of the hour
Effective action, the need of the day
We have to be competent to fight terrorism
If we want to neutralize it, come anything that may

Our, lack of, a united effort
Helps them, to survive `
Our lack of a cooperative strategy
Helps them thrive

Differences among nations
They exploit to the hilt
Systematically exploit our weakness
Legal governments they try to tilt

Massive illegal enterprises finance their cause
That we can't curb them, is a crying shame
Money laundering drug trafficking, gun running
All a part of the same game

Ammunition medicines, food
Loaded convoys to make the delivery
How they manage to cross checkpoints and barriers
Is certainly magical and devilry

Do something to get rid of this evil
Or they will take over for sure
All nations unite & cooperate to do it
There isn't any other cure

TERROR IN OUR MIDST

Suprio Ghosh

52. ALL NATIONS UNITE

Terrorists are joining hands
We know it's a fact
If we want to destroy the networks
It's now we have to act

Now is the time
The networks are still immature & 'Not old'
It's about time we neutralize them
Or we'll have miseries untold

Setting aside all differences
All nations ought to unite
Let's stop fighting each other
It's, terrorism, we've got to fight

While we are busy in petty squabbles
Our politics, wars and endless fuss
Our weaknesses & differences
The terrorists exploit, to annihilate us

They are technology savvy, dedicated & precise
It seems they have promises to keep
It seems that they are winning
While most governments talk, but sleep

They are zombies
Brainwashed to do an act
Their masters, sly & wicked
Who, handle them with tact

Suprio Ghosh

And unleash them upon
Civilized and harmonious societies
The obvious byproduct
Agony & chaos in endless varieties

Terrorists are joining hands
We know, it's a fact
If we want to neutralize them
It's now, we've got to act

Let us unite to fight terrorism
Setting aside all differences
Let us create amicable solutions
To get rid of all weaknesses

Cooperation among all nations is the only way
To win this perplexing war
And eventually heal humanity
Of, many an associated mental scar

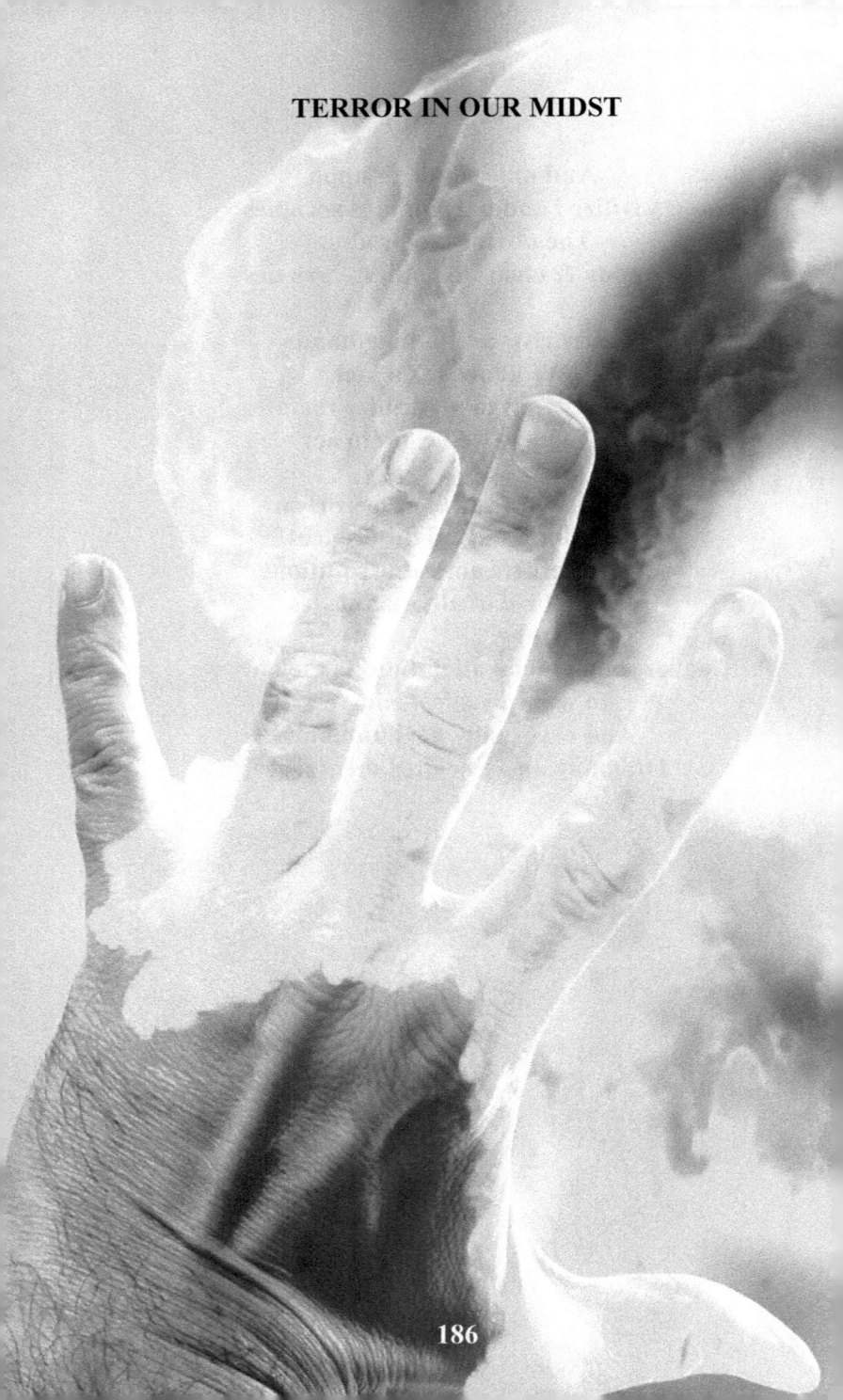

53. WHAT A WASTE OF BRAINWASHING TECHNIQUES?

Freedom doesn't mean
The media is free to misuse
To make a good sale
Controversial & shocking news choose

To make hay
While the sun shines
Not utilizing their power
Something on brainwashing lines

A power they can
Utilize to cure
The ills of society
And a lot more

To wipe out terrorism
To wipe out crime
To reorganize society
Into harmony and rhyme

To re-educate the people
So, no dropouts in society
Should be the media's
First and foremost priority

Someone's whims & notions
Waste others time
Misuse of such influential power
Is certainly a crime

TERROR IN OUR MIDST

Suprio Ghosh

**Freedom of the media
Doesn't mean free to misuse
To make a bumper sale
Sensationalize controversial & shocking news**

Suprio Ghosh

54. BETTER STRATEGIES PLEASE

The mighty powers are helpless
They don't know what to do
They are groping in the darkness
The leads are very few
Suicide bombers are giving sleepless nights
Is common and not anything new

They fight a faceless enemy
Who plays hide and seek
Who from deceptive covers, operate
And from obscure corners peek
They are just brainwashed zombies
Their wicked acts, of madness reek

No respect for life, prosperity or progress
Terrorizing the sane and the rational
Acts to destroy or deform the financial
The physical and the emotional
Striking lethal blows at will
Their ever growing numbers are phenomenal

They are usually seeking soft targets
The media makes their shocking acts sensational
The amount of coverage given to terrorism
Is much more than it deserves, really phenomenal
All that the media is interested in is
Bumper sales & benefits, the financial

Suprio Ghosh

Why do the mighty powers not win?
Are their strategies not right?
Do they not understand the enemy?
Whom they try to fight
Do they need a centralized info base command?
To win this international fight

Nations ought to share information
In order to set things right
Don't all nations understand?
That cooperation creates might
Don't all nations realize?`
It's a vicious & insane monster we all fight

Are their, 'Differences of opinion?'
Helping the evil cause
Are their decisions?
Illogical and full of flaws
Are most national external policies short sighted ideologies?
And helping this evil cause

Is no coordination and cooperation at the Global level?
Giving terrorism a breathing pause
Don't all nations see the obvious?
Terrorism is trying to destroy everything that is & was
Our strategies need rethinking
They are illogical and full of flaws

Their financers, their supporters & their suppliers
Ought to be in our net first
So that they have no ways and means
Of quenching their evil thirst
So that we can vanquish them quickly
An overnight victory, is a must

NO
PEN

Suprio Ghosh

55. LET'S TRY COOPERATION

Law makers & enforces
Seem to be stuck
We just might eradicate terrorism
With a bit of luck
We have to somehow
Get rid of this muck

We have to somehow be able to
Get rid of this evil
We have to nurture cooperation
And citizen, who are on the level
We need citizen who are
Cooperative & civil

So that this world is
A better place to live in
With lots of happiness
And less sin
With lots of tranquillity
And less din

Let's work together to achieve this goal
Let's eradicate evil & insanity
Let's save Planet Earth from destruction
To have peace & tranquillity
Save the birds, the bees, the insects & the trees
And eventually save humanity

Suprio Ghosh

56. HOW???

Terror strikes, communal violence
Each a senseless, ruthless act
Every sane being, for sure
Knows it's a fact

Then why does one take part
In such a senseless deed
Is there so much hate in us?
How do we crush its seed?

We have to do it
It's the need of the day
We have to do it
Come what may

Oh! Lord, help us
In this battle, to fight for sanity
Oh! Lord, help us
In this battle, to save humanity

TERROR IN OUR MIDST

Suprio Ghosh

57. DEAR GOD

Oh! God save the civilized world
From insane mayhem and terror
Help us to perceive the roots of this madness
So as to rectify any error
Help us to look within ourselves
See and act upon the image in the mirror

Save the civilized societies Oh! Lord
Save them from mayhem and terror
Are social systems so flawed?
Are they full of disparities and error?
Help us to rectify, the imperfect system
Cause discrimination and deprivation leads to terror

Oh! Lord, help us to correct
Policies that are wrong
Help us to end discrimination
So that people feel they belong
Help us to create healthy policies
Making Planet Earth into heaven and life a song